Karen Brown's
Switzerland

Charming Inns & Itineraries

Written by

KAREN BROWN and CLARE BROWN

Illustrations by Barbara Tapp
Cover Painting by Jann Pollard

Karen Brown's Guides, San Mateo, California

Karen Brown Titles

Austria: Charming Inns & Itineraries

California: Charming Inns & Itineraries

England: Charming Bed & Breakfasts

England, Wales & Scotland: Charming Hotels & Itineraries

France: Charming Bed & Breakfasts

France: Charming Inns & Itineraries

Germany: Charming Inns & Itineraries

Ireland: Charming Inns & Itineraries

Italy: Charming Bed & Breakfasts

Italy: Charming Inns & Itineraries

Mexico: Charming Inns & Itineraries

Mid-Atlantic: Charming Inns & Itineraries

New England: Charming Inns & Itineraries

Pacific Northwest: Charming Inns & Itineraries

Portugal: Charming Inns & Itineraries

Spain: Charming Inns & Itineraries

Switzerland: Charming Inns & Itineraries

In memory of
Michael
You will always be in our hearts

Cover painting: Hotel Alpenrose in the town of Wengen

Editors: Karen Brown, June Brown, Clare Brown, Kim Brown Holmsen, Anthony Brown, Debbie Tokumoto, Lorena Aburto Ramírez, Iris Sandilands, Courtney Gaviorno.

Illustrations: Barbara Tapp.

Cover painting: Jann Pollard.

Technical support: Michael Fiegel, Gary Meisner.

Maps: Michael Fiegel.

Copyright © 2004 by Karen Brown's Guides.

Distributed by Fodor's Travel Publications, Inc., 1745 Broadway, New York, NY 10019, USA.

Distributed in the United Kingdom by Random House UK, 20 Vauxhall Bridge Road, London, SW1V 2SA, England, phone: 44 20 7840 4000, fax: 44 20 7840 8406.

Distributed in Canada by Random House of Canada Limited, 2775 Matheson Blvd. East, Mississanga, Ontario, Canada L4W 4P7, phone: 905 624 0672, fax: 905 624 6217.

Distributed in Australia by Random House Australia, 20 Alfred Street, Milsons Point, Sydney NSW 2061, Australia, 2066, phone: 61 2 9954 9966, fax: 61 2 9954 4562.

Distributed in New Zealand by Random House New Zealand, 18 Poland Road, Glenfield, Auckland, New Zealand, phone: 64 9 444 7197, fax: 64 9 444 7524.

Distributed in South Africa by Random House South Africa, Endulani, East Wing, 5A Jubilee Road, Parktown 2193, South Africa, phone: 27 11 484 3538, fax: 27 11 484 6180.

A catalog record for this book is available from the British Library.

ISSN 1532-8791

Contents

We are proud to present
for our 2004 cover painting,
Hotel Alpenrose
in
Wengen.

Introduction

Switzerland is a country of incredible beauty: rugged mountain peaks enhanced by delicate, wispy clouds; velvety green meadows tucked high on mountain ledges; dramatic rivers rushing through narrow gorges; tiny blue lakes sparkling like jewels in their mountain pockets; postcard-worthy villages made up of toy-like chalets. The country is almost too perfect to be real. For centuries Switzerland has inspired poets and artists who have advertised her glories on paper and canvas and her reputation has attracted visitors from all over the world. Switzerland's tremendous growth in popularity as a tourist destination stems from the 19th century when the ever-hearty British, challenged by tales of unconquerable mountain peaks, ventured to Alpine villages in search of adventure. These sportsmen returned to England, spreading the word of the glories of Switzerland. One of these was Edward Whymper, a young English gentleman, who on July 14, 1865, at the young age of 20, came to Zermatt and conquered the summit of the Matterhorn. Whymper's enthusiasm is captured in his words of praise for the beauty of Switzerland:

*"However magnificent dreams of the imagination may be,
they always remain inferior to reality."*

About Switzerland

The Swiss call their country Helvetia and all federal documents bear the seal of the Confederation Helvetia, CH, or Swiss Confederation. Swiss independence dates from the days of William Tell when the magistrates from three cantons, then under Hapsburg rule, met to courageously and successfully oppose the hand of the ruling landholders. It was in 1291, on a meadow near Lake Lucerne, at the Rutli, that the magistrates set the seal to the new Confederation Helvetia. Those original three cantons, Uri, Schwyz, and Unterwalden, have expanded over the centuries into 26 cantons (23 if you do not consider the semi-cantons of Appenzell, Basel, and Unterwalden). Each jealously guards its autonomy and separate identity. The canton of Bern is the capital of Switzerland and serves as the seat of the federal government. However, the Swiss have historically shunned centralization of power and so, rather than have too many federal branches in one city, they maintain the supreme court at Lausanne.

Although Switzerland is a small country (barely 323 kilometers wide and 161 kilometers north to south), it has a compulsory military service, being determined to protect its hard-won independence, national character, and peace. Every young Swiss man must enlist at the age of 20 and complete 17 weeks of basic training. Then, until the age of 50 or 55 he is responsible for participating in a few weeks of annual "refresher" courses. This military force is always ready to defend the country and can be coordinated into action at a moment's notice. We often encountered such training groups who were "stationed" at our hotel. They would practice maneuvers by day then return to the hotel in the afternoon and often spend their leisure hours washing their Mercedes cars. The most humorous example of their presence, however, was at night when we would retire and find heavy combat boots lining the hall, left out to be polished. Where else but in Switzerland?

Contrary to the Swiss people's reputation of being somewhat aloof, we find them to be exceedingly cordial and hospitable. Not with a back-slapping brand of friendliness, but a friendliness wrapped in reserve and dignity—no less real though quite "proper." Perhaps the Swiss dedication to hard work, their total commitment to providing excellence of service, and their respect for privacy have been misinterpreted as "coldness."

AIRFARES

Karen Brown's Guides have long recommended Auto Europe for their excellent car rental services and we are now very pleased to introduce their air travel division, Destination Europe, to our readers. An airline broker working with major American and European carriers, Destination Europe offers deeply discounted coach- and business-class fares to over 200 European gateway cities. It also gives Karen Brown travelers an additional 5% discount off its already highly competitive prices. You can make reservations online via our website, *www.karenbrown.com* (click Discount Airfares on our home page), or at (800) 223-5555. When phoning, be sure to use the Karen Brown ID number 99006187 to secure your discount on the lowest prices they currently offer.

CAR RENTAL

Readers frequently ask our advice on car rental companies. We always use Auto Europe, a car rental broker that works with the major car rental companies to find the lowest possible price. They also offer motor homes and chauffeur services. Auto Europe's toll-free phone service from every European country connects you to their U.S.-based, 24-hour reservation center (ask for the card with European phone numbers to be sent to you). Auto Europe offers our readers a 5% discount, and occasionally free upgrades. Be sure to use the Karen Brown ID number 99006187 to receive your discount and any special offers. You can make your own reservations online via our website, *www.karenbrown.com* (select Auto Europe from the home page), or by telephone (800-223-5555).

CURRENCY

The Swiss franc (CHF) is the official currency of Switzerland. An increasingly popular and convenient way to obtain foreign currency is simply to use your bankcard at an ATM machine. You pay a fixed fee for this but, depending on the amount you withdraw, it is usually less than the percentage-based fee charged to exchange currency or travelers' checks. Be sure to check with your bank or credit card company about fees and necessary pin numbers prior to departure. Visit our website (*www.karenbrown.com*) for an easy-to-use online currency converter.

DRIVING

Roads, like everything else in Switzerland, are efficiently marked. Once you get used to the excellent color-coded sign system, directions are easy to follow: green signs indicate motorways, blue signs mark regular roads, white signs depict the smaller roads, and yellow signs mark walking paths or roads closed to vehicle traffic. Most of the roads are excellent, but some of the smaller roads in remote areas, i.e., narrow, twisting, mountain passes, are not recommended for the faint of heart. It is also notable that certain passes close during the winter months. To inquire about road conditions while driving in Switzerland, you can reach a hot line by dialing 163.

DRIVER'S LICENSE: A valid driver's license from your own country is sufficient when driving within Switzerland.

DRUNK DRIVING: The penalties for driving while under the influence of alcohol are very severe. Do not drink and drive.

GASOLINE: The price of gasoline in Switzerland is very high so be sure to budget for this when making your plans. If you find yourself short of cash, many of the service stations (such as BP, ESSO, and Shell) will accept payment by a major credit card. Some of the service stations have an efficient system whereby you put coins into an appropriate slot and can pump your own gas—day or night. Some service stations are even more automated and you can purchase gas by inserting your credit card directly into the indicated slot. Service stations off the major freeways frequently close for a few hours in the middle of the day.

MOTORWAYS: Switzerland does not collect tolls on its motorways—instead, motorists must buy a permit (to be displayed on the windshield) in order to drive on them. If you rent a car in Switzerland, the rental company will have done this for you. If you are arriving from another country, you can buy a permit (called a *vignette*) at the border.

ROAD CONDITIONS: Highways link Switzerland's major cities and are kept in remarkably good condition. No sooner are the snows melting in the spring sun than maintenance crews begin repairing damage done by winter weather. Many villages are tucked away in remote valleys linked to civilization by narrow little roads, but even these are well tended by the efficient Swiss and are usually in good condition.

ROAD SIGNS: If you are driving, prepare yourself before leaving home by learning the international road signs so that you can obey all the rules and avoid the hazard and embarrassment of heading the wrong way down a small street or parking in a forbidden zone. There are several basic sign shapes: triangular signs warn that there is danger ahead; circular signs indicate compulsory rules and information; square signs give information concerning telephones, parking, camping, etc.

SEAT BELTS: Seat belts are mandatory when driving within Switzerland. It is also the law that babies and small children must ride in proper car seats.

SPEED LIMITS: There are speed limits throughout Switzerland: motorways—maximum speed 120 kilometers per hour (kph); highways—maximum speed 80 kph; towns and built-up areas—maximum speed 50 kph.

ELECTRICITY

If you are taking any electrical appliances made for use in the United States, you will need a transformer plus a two-pin adapter. A voltage of 220 AC at 50 cycles per second is almost countrywide, though in remote areas you may encounter 120V. The voltage is often displayed on the socket. Even though we recommend that you purchase appliances with dual-voltage options whenever possible, you will still need the appropriate socket adapter. Also, be especially careful with expensive equipment such as computers—verify with the manufacturer the adapter/converter capabilities and requirements.

FESTIVALS

Proud of their local traditions and cultures, the Swiss observe many festivals and events that serve as reminders of the past. They range from centuries-old ceremonies commemorating national victories to popular pageants and processions. Colorful costumes, often unique to a particular canton, are frequently worn on Sundays and festive occasions. Music and theater are important in Swiss life—from the theater and symphony in the larger cities to the local band or yodeling society in the villages, throughout the year the Swiss host numerous festivals incorporating music. Festivals and traditions inspired by the seasons are also plentiful and fun to experience. To name a few: in early summer in the Engadine, farmers in traditional costumes parade their cattle adorned with heavy old cow bells through the villages to higher summer pastures. In the fall, gaiety prevails with the grape harvest in the numerous wine regions. In summer, special sports contests take place, such as Alpine wrestling, tugs-of-war, or *hornet*, a team game in which a vulcanite disc is "swatted" with a wooden racket. Political meetings are also staged as a traditional event. In spring, there are open-air cantonal meetings, *Landsgemeinden*, held by citizens in the cantons of Appenzell, Glarus, and Unterwalden. In the town square of each canton, elections take place and issues are debated and voted upon by uplifted hand. Switzerland Tourism is an excellent source for festival information.

FLY LUGGAGE

In a total commitment to ease the way for the traveler, Swissair has devised an ingenious, outstandingly convenient method for the handling of your luggage which they call "Fly Luggage." From over 100 train or postal-bus stations throughout Switzerland you can check your luggage via the Geneva or Zürich airport all the way to your own hometown airport. (Of course, you will need to follow the customs procedures of luggage inspection at your gateway city.) All you need is a plane ticket with a confirmed reservation for a scheduled flight on Swissair from Zürich or Geneva. The cost is nominal and is per piece of luggage (approximately $18 each piece). If you have a railway ticket to the Zürich or

Geneva airport, you pay even less. Please allow sufficient time—inquire at the local train stations about time requirements for checking in your luggage. Similarly, when arriving at either of these airports, you can check your luggage right through to your destination and climb aboard the train completely unencumbered.

FOOD & WINE

Switzerland is bordered by Germany, Austria, Italy, and France. Culinary specialties from each of these countries have been absorbed into the Swiss kitchens where talented chefs interpret these various foods into gourmet delights.

Many guide books imply that Swiss cooking is mediocre—that it has no character or style of its own. We feel that this is totally unfair. The high degree of training stressed in the Swiss hotel schools contributes to the consistently fine food and service that is found not only in the elegant city restaurants, but also in tiny restaurants in remote hamlets. Usually every entree is cooked to order—rarely will you see a steam table. For a grand finale to your meal, Swiss pastries and desserts are world-famous.

You will find throughout your travels in Switzerland delicious fruits and vegetables from the garden, a marvelous selection of fresh fish from the rivers and lakes, outstanding veal dishes, and wicked desserts followed by an assortment of local cheeses.

To satisfy the morning appetite, the breakfast repast is usually a Continental offering of rolls, bread, butter, jelly, cheese, and Muesli, served with coffee or tea. At larger hotels, you can often order as a supplement and for an additional charge juices, eggs, and breakfast meats.

The following list of Swiss specialties is not comprehensive—it is merely a sampling of some of the delicacies we most enjoyed while in Switzerland. The fun of completing the list is left to your own culinary adventures.

BRATWURST: I am sure the Swiss would chuckle to see included such mundane fare as Bratwurst in a specialty food list. However, there is nothing more delicious than the plump grilled veal Swiss hot dogs smothered in onions, topped by mustard, and accompanied by fried potatoes. A cold beer makes this meal memorable.

BÜNDNERFLEISCH: In southeastern Switzerland, the Grisons area, an unusual air-dried beef or ham cut into wafer-thin slices is served as a delicacy.

CHEESES: Switzerland is famous for her cheeses. Appenzell and Gruyères are but two of the many towns that produce these mouth-watering cheeses. You will find that each area seems to produce its own variety of cheese.

CHOCOLATE: This list would not be complete without the mention of Swiss chocolate. Nestlé, Tobler, or simply "Swiss" are synonymous with the world's best chocolate. Rarely does a suitcase return home without a candy bar or two tucked into the corner.

FONDUE: The Swiss specialty of fondue has gained popularity all over the world. Melted Gruyères cheese, white wine, garlic, and kirsch are brought hot to the table in a chafing dish and diners use long forks to dip squares of bread into the delectable mixture. Fondue Bourguignonne, chunks of meat skewered on forks and fried in oil and seasoned at will, is also popular throughout the country.

FRITURE DE PERCHETTES: Nothing could be more superb than the tiny, mild fillet of fresh perch fried in oil found on most menus during the summer in the Lake Geneva area. Be sure to try this outstanding gourmet delight.

GESCHNETZLETS: Veal is very popular in Switzerland. Perhaps the most famous and delicious method of preparation is small pieces cooked in a white wine sauce with mushrooms. This is frequently called Veal Zürich on the menu.

HERO JAM: This divine jam comes in many delicious fruit and berry flavors and is traditionally served with little hard rolls that break into quarters.

LECKERLI: This is a spicy, cake-like, ginger-flavored cookie covered with a thin sugar icing. To be really good, the cookie must "snap" when broken.

RACLETTE: Raclette is a fun dish, a countryman's dinner and feast. A block of Bagnes cheese is split and melted over a fire. The softened cheese, scraped onto your plate, is most often served with potatoes and onions. Sometimes variations in the accompaniment are offered, such as the addition of mushrooms, tomatoes, ham, and sausage—almost as you would order variations of an omelet or quiche.

ROSCHTI or RÖSTI: These delicious fried potatoes are served throughout Switzerland, often accompanying sausages and roasts. The potatoes are diced and lightly browned in butter—frequently with the addition of diced onions.

WINES: To complement the meal, Switzerland produces some exceptional wines that are rarely exported—a definite loss to the rest of the world. Many of these wines are made from grapes grown in the Rhône Valley and have a light, slightly fruity taste and a tinge of effervescence. Be sure to take the opportunity to sample Swiss wines. If you want to economize, ask your waiter if he has an *offenen wein,* an "open" wine served either in a carafe or a bottle without a cork.

GEOGRAPHY

The unique geography of Switzerland lends itself to breathtaking beauty. In the northwestern section of Switzerland are the Jura Mountains while 60% of the southeast of the country is dominated by the Alps. In between these two mountainous areas, the verdant lowlands sweep from Lake Geneva diagonally across the country to Lake Constance. You return home with the impression of precipitous Alpine peaks, deep mountain gorges, beautiful mountain valleys, glaciers gleaming in the sun, glorious blue lakes, spectacular waterfalls, gently flowing rivers, soft rolling hills, picturesque villages, toy-like churches, and quaint chalets. Every turn in the road offers postcard vistas for your scrapbook of memories.

LANGUAGES

Switzerland is a country of four languages: German is spoken all over central and northern Switzerland; Italian is spoken in the south; French is spoken in the west; and Romansch is spoken by a small number of people in the southeast. English is usually spoken in the hotels and shops in tourist centers. In remote areas you might need to communicate using a dictionary and a smile.

If you enjoy diversity, in the course of a day you will find your skills challenged with multiple languages. Quite surprisingly, you can travel a distance of just a few kilometers, from one village to the next, and find yourself in a new region and encounter a complete change in language. If you are uncertain upon arrival in a given town as to whether to use your French or German skills, road and town signs are an excellent clue.

Languages of Switzerland

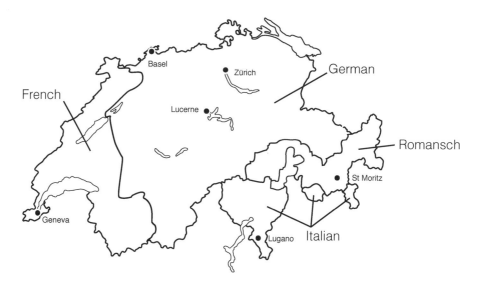

Introduction–About Switzerland

RESTAURANTS

Switzerland boasts some of Europe's most outstanding restaurants. An exceptionally high degree of professionalism and excellence is maintained in even the simplest of restaurants, and the presentation and quality of food rival any in the world. Many restaurants in Switzerland serve food piping hot from a cart—a nicety usually encountered in only the most exclusive restaurants elsewhere. Then, when you have finished your entree, you are presented with a comparable second portion, brought to you on a clean warm plate with the same skillful delivery.

Many inns have two restaurants. Frequently there is a central entry hall with a somewhat formal restaurant on one side and a "pub-like," informal restaurant on the other. The latter is called the *stubli,* and if you are in the countryside, this is where the farmers gather in the late afternoon for a bit of farm gossip and perhaps a card game of *jass.* Locals gather after work in the *stubli* for relaxation, and in the evening families congregate for a glass of beer, wine, or a thimbleful of kirsch.

SHOPPING

Switzerland has a tempting array of products to entice even the reluctant buyer. Shopping in Switzerland is fun: the stores are pretty and the merchandise is usually of excellent quality.

Many larger towns have stores that feature an exceptional selection of art and handicraft items, referred to as *Heimatwerk*, from the surrounding region. (While in Zürich visit the *Schweizer Heimatwerk*, a marvelous store that features crafts from all regions—you will find it on the Limmat Quai just across from the train station.) In Switzerland the prices are usually set, so there is no bargaining, and tax is included.

Some shopping suggestions: watches, clocks, mechanical toys, wood carvings, hand-painted pottery, cow bells, Swiss army knives, chocolates, cheeses, kirsch, antiques, Saint Gallen lace, hand-embroidered items, fine cottons, children's clothing, and ski wear.

SPORTS

Sports are part of the lure of Switzerland. The mountains have been tempting climbers since the middle of the 1800s when Edward Whymper crossed the Channel from England to be the first to reach the top of the famous Matterhorn. Ski areas such as Zermatt, Saint Moritz, Davos, Wengen, Klosters, Villars, and Verbier are world-famous. Mountain lakes such as Lake Geneva, Lake Lucerne, and Lake Zürich are ideal for boating, fishing, and swimming. Marked walking trails beckon hikers from far and near and the skies of the mountain valleys are often colored with the canvas of hang-gliders.

SWITZERLAND TOURISM

Switzerland Tourism, previously known as the Swiss National Tourist Office, is an excellent source of information. If you have any questions not answered in this guide, or need special information concerning a particular destination within Switzerland, they will be glad to assist you. Also, you can visit their web site: *www.myswitzerland.ch.*

Switzerland Tourism, Head Office
P.O. Box 695
CH-8027 Zürich, Switzerland
tel: (01) 288 11 11; fax: (01) 288 12 05

Switzerland Tourism
Worldwide toll-free number
tel: (011) 800-100-200-30
e-mail: info.int@switzerland.com

Switzerland Tourism
608 Fifth Avenue, Swiss Center
New York, New York l0020-2303
tel: (212) 757-5944; fax: (212) 262-6116

Switzerland Tourism
Telephone contacts only:
San Francisco, CA, tel: (415) 362-2260
toll-free in US: 877-794-8037

Switzerland Tourism
Swiss Center, 10 Wardour Street
London W1D 6QF, England
tel: (020) 7734 1921; fax: (020) 7437 4577

Switzerland Tourism
926 The East Mall
Etobicoke, Ontario M9B 6KI, Canada
tel: (416) 695-2090; fax: (416) 695-2774

TELEPHONES

CALLS TO SWITZERLAND: If you want to make a call to Switzerland from the United States, dial 011 (the international access code), 41, Switzerland's country code, then the city code (dropping the initial 0), and then the local telephone number.

CALLS WITHIN SWITZERLAND: There are many public telephone booths conveniently located throughout Switzerland. To use a public phone you need to purchase a Taxcard priced at CHF 5, 10, or 20 at a post office, rail station, newsstand, gas station, or hotel. Instructions for using the card are displayed in the phone booths. For calling a local number, omit the city code (the numbers in the parenthesis). For calling a long-distance number, dial the city code, complete with the 0, and the number.

CALLS FROM SWITZERLAND: Long-distance calls from Switzerland are expensive. Use your telephone credit card such as AT&T or Sprint to make calls to the United States. Before leaving home, find out the telephone number in Switzerland that connects you directly to the United States.

CELLPHONES: Cellphones are wonderful to have as some hotels do not have direct-dial phones in the guestrooms. Also, cellphones are enormously convenient when you are on the road and want to call for directions or advise of a changed arrival.

Cellphones can be rented through your car rental company and at the airport or train stations, or you can purchase an international phone once overseas. If you are considering taking your cellphone from home, be sure to check with your carrier to make sure that your phone even has international capability. Sometimes it is necessary to make arrangements in advance of your departure to activate a special service. We would also recommend getting international phone access numbers and inquiring about international access charges or rates so there are no billing surprises.

TRANSPORTATION

Although cars afford the flexibility to deviate on a whim and explore enticing side roads or beckoning hilltop villages, Switzerland's transportation network is so superb that you can travel conveniently by train, boat, or bus throughout the country—from the largest city to the smallest hamlet. So, if you were ever thinking of a vacation without a car, this is the place to try it. The ingenuity of the network is almost beyond belief: the schedules are so finely tuned that buses, trains, and boats all interconnect. Not only do the time schedules jibe perfectly, but usually you can walk from where the boat arrives to the train or bus station. It is like a puzzle, and great fun.

Should you be planning an extensive holiday using the Swiss public transportation system, there is an invaluable set of books called the Official Timetable, published once a year, which contains a wealth of information, outlining every timetable within Switzerland for boats, trains, and buses. There are other train guides published, but this official guide is the only one we found that shows access by public transportation to every town—no matter how tiny or how isolated. Unfortunately, you can no longer purchase the Official Timetable in the USA; however, it is available at train stations and kiosks in Switzerland. The Eurail Timetable Guide is available free of charge through Rail Europe—visit our website, *www.karenbrown.com*, and click on Rail Europe. The Thomas Cook European Rail Timetable lists rail and some ferry and bus schedules in tourist destinations, tel: (800) 367-7984.

BOATS: Switzerland is a land of lakes and rivers and to travel the country by its waterways affords an entirely new and enchanting perspective. Often a river boat or lake steamer will depart from a dock just a few meters from a hotel, enabling you to journey from one destination to another or continue inland by connecting with either a train, bus, or hired car. Concerned with preserving their heritage, the Swiss have refurbished a number of beautiful and graceful lake steamers and ferries so that you can not only see Switzerland by water, but also experience some nostalgia.

BUSES: Boasting more mileage than the Swiss railway itself, the postal bus lines originated after World War I with the primary purpose of transporting mail. In conjunction with the entire network of railway lines, every village in Switzerland is serviced by postal bus—providing Switzerland with one of the most exceptional transportation networks in the world. Depending on the demand, there are 4- to 5-person limousines, mini-buses, or the ever familiar buttercup-yellow buses. In addition to the mail, the bus lines are responsible for transporting about 15 million passengers. Their dependability and excellence of service is impressive.

In Switzerland, the position of postal bus driver is very prestigious. Those chosen for the job are unmatched in driving ability. Their record is faultless—in the history of the postal bus service there has not been one fatal accident. In addition to excellent driving techniques, the drivers also play an important role in the community—usually they are well versed on the local news and social activities and familiar with the most recent wedding, gossip, or current business venture. Bus drivers must know every millimeter of the road, and their training is exacting and stringent. Thousands apply each year for positions available to just a few. To qualify, an applicant must be no older than 28, have completed his military duty, pass a rigorous physical exam, and be able to speak three languages. They undergo years of specialized training before taking position behind the wheel. Their first assignment is to drive a postal truck, then a bus in the lowlands, and as a finale they must negotiate a bus up a treacherous, narrow, mountain road, and then successfully complete a seemingly impossible U-turn, observed and judged by a busload of veteran bus drivers. Justifiably, those who achieve the position of postal driver have command of the roadways and other vehicles are expected to yield. It is not uncommon to see a postal busman assisting a petrified driver who has encountered difficulty on a pass or a narrow bend and who is too frightened to move. The sound of their horn, as the postal buses wind up the incredible mountain passes, warning other vehicles of their approach, may seem familiar. Indeed, it is a melody from Rossini's *William Tell Overture.*

TAXIS: Unless money doesn't matter, try when possible to avoid taxis while in Switzerland—they are very expensive. Frequently you can take a bus or tram from the train station almost to the door of your hotel. If you are on a tight budget, when you make your room reservation, ask the manager or owner if there is a direct bus or tram from the station to your hotel. If so, ask the number of the bus or tram, name of the place to get off, and how many stops it is from the station. If you have a map and luggage on wheels that you can pull, another alternative is to walk.

TRAINS: Switzerland has one of the most remarkable rail systems in the world, with more than 5,500 kilometers of track. Just over half are operated by the Swiss Federal Railway system while the others are privately owned. However, they are all integrated and connections are scheduled to synchronize both efficiently and conveniently. Their timetable is patterned after the perfection of the Swiss clock—trains depart on the scheduled second.

If you are flying into either Zürich or Geneva, you will find a beautifully geared network: from either of these airports you can board a train directly to many of the tourist destinations throughout Switzerland. The entire setup is wonderfully convenient for the traveler. As you exit the baggage claim area, there is a counter where you can check your luggage right through to your destination and climb aboard the train completely unencumbered. If you really want to spoil yourself, when the train arrives at your first night's stop, you can take a cab to your hotel, give the baggage claim ticket to the receptionist and ask him or her to send the porter to the station for your bags.

The train stations, often chalet-style buildings, are spotlessly clean, and quite frequently double as a residence for the station master. You often find evidence of domesticity—flowers cascading from the upstairs windowboxes and laundry hanging on the line. Station masters are handsome in their uniforms and most speak some English.

Train Tips: It is very important to be able to quickly find "your" train as the schedules mesh like clockwork. Once you have the system down pat, you won't panic when you see that there are only a few minutes to get from one train to the other. You will know that this has been established as enough time to make the connection. In every station a large yellow poster with black print lists all the outgoing trains according to departure times. You need to study your own map because where you want to disembark might not appear on the sign—you might need to look at a major city beyond where you plan to get off. Along with the schedule, the yellow sign also states the number of the track from which each train  will depart. Large white signs with black print show the arrival times of trains. When you go to the departure track, there is a diagram showing the alignment of the cars so that you can stand at the proper spot for first- or second-class cars. This diagram is very important because on certain routes, trains split and different cars go to different cities.

If you plan to travel by train in Europe, you can research schedules and fares and even purchase tickets and passes online. (Note that many special fares and passes are available only if purchased outside Switzerland.) For information and the best possible fares, and to book tickets online, visit our website, *www.karenbrown.com*.

TRANSPORTATION PASSES

Public transportation is easy and economical to use. It is an absolute joy to be able to just climb aboard a train on a whim or to hop on one of the numerous boats that ply Switzerland's many lakes. Even if you are traveling by car, you might well want to take some sightseeing excursions by train since they whisk you right to the center of the towns. From Zürich take a quick trip to Schaffhausen to see the Rheinfall, or an excursion to Winterthur to see the superb Oskar Reinhart museum.

There are train passes that can be purchased outside Switzerland through travel agents. All passes are priced for either first- or second-class travel—if you are not on a tight budget, you might want to go first class since these sections are less crowded and more comfortable. Swiss rail tickets and passes are available through Rail Europe (see page 15). Following are some of the available passes—one surely tailored with you in mind.

SWISS PASS: The Swiss Pass entitles you to unlimited trips on the entire network of the Swiss transportation system covering 14,500 kilometers of railroad, boat, and postal bus routes, as well as streetcars and buses in 36 Swiss cities—plus a 25% discount on excursions to most mountaintops. The pass is available for 4, 8, 15, 21 days or 1 month of consecutive travel.

SWISS FLEXI PASS: The Swiss Flexi Pass might be perfect for you if you are on a driving vacation. It has the same benefits as the Swiss Pass, but is more flexible. You can choose any three days of travel within a one-month period.

SWISS CARD: The Swiss Card, valid for one month, entitles you to a transfer from a Swiss airport or border point to any destination in Switzerland, and a second transfer from any destination in Switzerland to a Swiss airport or border point. It also allows unlimited trips on all other train, bus, and steamer services at half fare. (This card is not quite as convenient because you need to purchase a ticket before boarding your train, bus, boat, or tram.)

SWISS FAMILY TRAVEL PLAN: Children under 16 travel free if accompanied by at least one parent with a Swiss Pass, Flexi Pass, or Swiss Card. Request the family card when ordering your ticket. Note: Some of the major intercity trains have a playroom car where children can romp and play to their hearts' content.

TRANSPORTATION—SPECIAL EXCURSIONS

Switzerland has packaged some marvelous excursions by public transportation that make travel a real adventure. Perhaps in no other country are there so many possibilities to enjoy sightseeing this way. Some of the choices are listed below.

The BERNINA EXPRESS sets out from Chur and Lanquart and climbs over the Bernina Pass at 2253 meters before dropping down to Tirano, Italy, a picturesque town of Mediterranean influence. Along the way, the dramatic journey takes you through five loop tunnels and two normal tunnels and over eight viaducts. You can take an air-conditioned coach from Tirano on to Lugano.

The GLACIER EXPRESS links Zermatt and Saint Moritz. The incredible, 7½-hour adventure on the quaint bright-red train crosses 291 bridges, goes through 91 tunnels, and chugs over the Oberalppass and the Albulapass. Lunch is served en route in a nostalgic, old-fashioned, paneled dining car. Reservations can be made in the USA through Rail Europe (see page 15).

The PALM EXPRESS, an all-day adventure by bus, begins in Saint

Moritz and loops south to Lake Lugano. (Note: It no longer continues on to Zermatt.) En route the landscape changes from glaciers to palm trees. For reservations contact the booking office in Saint Moritz, tel: (081) 837 67 64, fax: (081) 837 67 60, or in Lugano, tel: (091) 807 85 20, fax: (091) 923 69 39.

The WILLIAM TELL EXPRESS links Central Switzerland with the Swiss-Italian Lake District. You board a nostalgic paddle steamer in Lucerne and cruise to Flüelen, enjoying en route a gourmet meal in the first-class restaurant. In Flüelen, a train is waiting and the trip continues through the Reuss Valley, through the 15-kilometer Gotthard Tunnel, and on to Bellinzona. From here, you can continue on either to Lugano or Locarno. Advance reservations are mandatory. They can be made through your travel agent, through Rail Europe (see page 15) or in Switzerland at any train station. Reservations can be made no more than two months and no less than two weeks prior to the travel date.

TRIP CANCELLATION INSURANCE

Because unexpected medical or personal emergencies—or other situations beyond our control—sometimes result in the need to alter or cancel travel plans, we strongly recommend travel insurance. Prepaid travel expenses such as airline tickets, car rentals, and train fares are not always refundable and most hotels and bed and breakfasts will expect payment of some, if not all of your booking, even in an emergency. While the owners might be sympathetic, many of the properties in our guides have relatively few rooms, so it is difficult for them to absorb the cost of a cancellation. A link on our website (*www.karenbrown.com*) will connect you to a variety of insurance policies that can be purchased online.

WEATHER

For such a tiny nation, Switzerland offers an amazing variety of climates: the brisk mountain weather is quite different from the milder temperatures encountered near Lake Geneva or the balmy Swiss-Italian Lake District. Because of the sudden, unpredictable weather changes, it is highly recommended that you use the so-called "onion principle" in clothing. Wear layers of clothing, like T-shirts, sweaters, and jackets, which you can take off or put on at any given time to adjust to the weather conditions. Also be sure to pack good, comfortable walking shoes (there are lots of cobblestoned streets) and suntan lotion for summer and winter vacations.

The seasons in Switzerland are varied and all are lovely. Winter beckons the sports enthusiasts with excellent downhill ski slopes, beautifully marked cross-country trails, skating, and curling. Winter is also for those who simply love the charm of picture-book villages wrapped in blankets of snow. Spring is my favorite time of year. Weather in late spring can be absolutely glorious—the meadows are a symphony of color with a profusion of wildflowers, and the mountains still have their winter cap of snow. Summer is the most popular season. The days are usually mild and sunny and the mountain passes are open so you can explore all the isolated mountain villages. Autumn is lovely, with the first snowstorms leaving the mountains wearing new bonnets of pristine snow. The trees and vineyards are mellowing in shades of red and gold and the flowers are at their peak of bloom in every windowbox. There is a hint of winter in the air, except in the Swiss-Italian Lake District where the weather is usually still balmy.

About Itineraries

We have put together five itineraries for Switzerland, each highlighting the entire country rather than a particular region and each designed around an individual theme. *Mountain Adventures* explores some of Switzerland's most spectacular mountain villages and settings. *Medieval Switzerland* traces a journey through Switzerland's most enchanting walled towns and medieval villages. Saturated with history and a romantic past, this itinerary steps into an era of knights, chivalry, castles, cobblestoned streets, wenches, jousting, jesters, turrets, and bows and arrows. *Best on a Budget* travels the popular route south from Zürich to Lucerne, Interlaken, and the mountains, then dips along the Italian border to the Lake District and then into the beautiful Engadine Valley before circling back to Zürich. Accommodation in Switzerland is relatively expensive when compared to other countries in Europe but for this itinerary we have selected traditional Swiss inns whose simplicity of accommodation is reflected in the price. You can experience the beauty of Switzerland on a budget and not compromise comfort or charm. *Switzerland by Train, Boat & Bus* takes advantage of the country's fabulous transportation network and lets you most effectively soak in the splendors of Switzerland's valleys, mountains, rivers, and lakes without having to attempt the roads and passes in your own car. Most of Switzerland's highlights are incorporated into this romantic itinerary. *Swiss Highlights,* an introduction to the major cities and popular destinations, is written for the first-time traveler to Switzerland.

With the exception of *Switzerland by Train, Boat & Bus*, these itineraries are designed to be traveled by car. There is no better way to explore the countryside, to really understand the depths and reaches of a valley, to fully comprehend the dimensions, magnificence, and power of lofty Alpine peaks, and to experience the beauty and grace of lakes and rivers. Cars are easy to rent and available in most mid-sized towns and driving is on the "proper" side.

The five suggested itineraries in this guide crisscross back and forth across Switzerland. Because certain "key" destinations reappear in several itineraries we decided to describe them once in detail in a reference section, entitled *Sightseeing Reference*, rather than elaborate on them over and over again in each itinerary. This section begins on page 33.

ITINERARY MAPS

Each itinerary is preceded by a map showing the route and each hotel listing is referenced on its top line to a map at the back of the book. To make it easier for you, hotel location maps are divided into a grid of four parts—a, b, c, and d—as indicated on each map's key. All maps are an artist's renderings and are not intended to replace detailed commercial maps. We recommend the Michelin overview map of Switzerland, Michelin Map 729 (1 cm = 4 km) and suggest you use highlight pens to outline your route. You can purchase Michelin Maps from our website, *www.karenbrown.com*.

About Hotels

Charm and old-world ambiance are used as the basis for the selection of hotels in this guide. Some of our recommendations are luxuriously elegant, while others are quite simple. Some are located in the center of cities, while others are tucked into remote mountain villages. Our hotels vary also in quality. Frankly, some are better than others because in a few instances we have chosen a hotel not on its merits alone, but so that you would have a place to stay in a region or village we considered so spectacular that it warranted an overnight. We have indicated what each hotel has to offer and have described the setting for your consideration. We believe that if you know what to expect, you will not be disappointed. Therefore, we have tried always to be candid and honest in our appraisals. The charm of a simple countryside chalet will beckon some while a sophisticated, luxurious city hotel will appeal to others. For a few lucky travelers, price is never a factor if the hotel is outstanding. For others, budget will guide their choice. Read each description carefully so that you can select the hotel that most suits you.

CREDIT CARDS

Whether or not an establishment accepts credit cards is indicated in the list of icons at the bottom of each description by the symbol ▣. We have also specified in the bottom details which cards are accepted as follows: AX–American Express, MC–MasterCard, VS–Visa, or simply, all major. Note: Even if an inn does not accept credit card payment, it will perhaps request your account number as a guarantee of arrival.

DATES OPEN

Under each hotel's description we have indicated when the hotel is open. Some hotels close the end of July until the middle of August—more commonly, many close during the spring and again in the fall. This is especially true in mountain resorts that are open for skiing in the winter then close for maintenance in the spring in anticipation of the influx of summer tourists. A word of caution: Even though many hotels quote a certain date to open or close, in reality it might fluctuate by a day or two, perhaps because of weather and occupancy. So it is always wise to contact the hotels if you are traveling footloose and without reservations to confirm that they are open before you head over that mountain pass on the assumption that you'll find a bed—particularly if your travels coincide with the beginning or end of a season.

DECOR

Regardless of the category of Swiss hotel, service and quality of cuisine are generally stressed over the importance of decor. The old-world charm is usually allocated to the public and dining areas, while the bedrooms are simple and modern, with light knotty-pine furniture. Rarely do you find an inn with antique decor in the bedrooms.

Often the most appealing room in the inn is the *stubli*, a cozy dining room where the local villagers congregate in the evening for a drink and conversation. As a general rule, the *stubli* oozes with the charm of mellow wood paneling, rustic carved chairs, and pretty country curtains.

DINING OPTIONS

Many of the inns featured in this guide have a restaurant (sometimes just for the use of guests) and offer the option of demi-pension, which means that breakfast and dinner are included in the price of the room. We recommend that you accept this meal plan whenever it is available. Naturally, the nightly rate is higher, but, almost without exception, it is a very good value. When making a reservation ask if you can have demi-pension and the price. (Remember that usually demi-pension is quoted per person, so be sure you understand whether the rate is for one or two persons.) Each hotel has its own policy: some will provide demi-pension only with a minimum of a three-night stay; others offer the option from the first night—especially if requested in advance.

The type of menu with demi-pension varies: most hotels offer a set menu each night, but a few (usually the more deluxe hotels) offer a choice for the entree. There is sometimes a separate dining room for house guests who are staying on the demi-pension plan. Usually you have the same table each night, which is an advantage as you can get to know your neighbors. Another advantage—if you don't finish your bottle of wine, it will be saved and appear at your table the next night. Note: There are a few hotels in our guide that offer *only* demi-pension and, in that case, we have indicated that under the hotel's description. Although most hotels quote demi-pension on a per-person basis, for consistency purposes, we quote the per night cost for two persons sharing a double room.

ICONS

Icons allow us to provide additional information about our recommended properties. When using our website to supplement the guides, positioning the cursor over an icon will in many cases give you further details. For easy reference an icon key can be found on the last page of the book.

We have introduced these icons in the guidebooks and there are more on our website, *www.karenbrown.com.* ❄ Air conditioning in rooms, ⚓ Beach nearby, ▣ Breakfast included in room rate, ⚗ Children welcome, ♨ Cooking classes offered, ▦ Credit cards accepted, ☎ Direct-dial telephone in room, ⌂ Dogs by special request, ▥ Elevator, ⚚ Exercise room, ⚑ Mini-refrigerator in rooms, P Parking available, ❚❚ Restaurant, ⊘ Some non-smoking rooms, ✻ Spa, ≋ Swimming pool, ⚡ Tennis, ▦ Television with English channels, ⚘ Wedding facilities, ⚒ Wheelchair friendly, ⚐ Golf course nearby, ⚏ Hiking trails nearby, ⚞ Horseback riding nearby, ⚴ Skiing nearby, ⚓ Water sports nearby, ⚑ Wineries nearby.

FINDING HOTELS

To assist you in determining the general region in which a town where we recommend a hotel is located, one of the last lines of each hotel description refers to the town's canton (listed as "region"). At the back of the book, on page 229, you will find a map outlining Switzerland's cantons. After the canton map is a key map of Switzerland followed by six regional maps pinpointing each recommended hotel's location. The pertinent regional map number is given at the right on the top line of each hotel's description. To make it easier for you, we have divided each map into a grid of four parts—a, b, c, and d—as shown in the maps' key. Each hotel's description also indicates at the bottom its location with reference to neighboring, larger cities and gives the number of a specific regional Michelin map.

HOTELIERS

From large hotels to small inns, the owners' dedication and personal involvement in the management of their hotels are astounding. No job ever seems too small or inconsequential to merit attention. It is not unusual to find hoteliers supervising both the hotel and the restaurant—more often than not, we would discover the owner in the kitchen, dusting flour off his apron before extending a welcoming handshake. Swiss hoteliers, many having studied in their country's own prestigious hotel and restaurant schools, take great pride in their profession, and ownership is often passed down within a family from one generation to the next.

MEMBERSHIP AFFILIATIONS

A number of properties recommended in our guides also belong to private membership organizations. These associations impose their own criteria for selection and membership standards and have established a reputation for the particular type of property they include. One affiliation that is very well recognized throughout Europe is Relais & Châteaux and a number of properties that we recommend are members. We are familiar with their selection process, criteria, and membership standards and we feel comfortable in recommending this prestigious association to our readers. If a property that we recommend is also a member of the Relais & Châteaux group, we note that in the bottom details of the hotel description.

RATES

Rates, in Swiss francs (abbreviated to CHF), are those given to us for the 2004 high season. Switzerland is not part of the European Union and therefore does not use the euro. We quote the range of rates for two people sharing a double room, including taxes and service charges. If breakfast is included you will see the ☕ symbol in the list of icons at the bottom of each description. We point out the few cases where you are also required to eat dinner or lunch in house (demi-pension). Please use the rates we give as a guideline and be certain to ask what the rate is when you make a reservation. Please visit our website (*www.karenbrown.com*) for an easy-to-use online currency converter.

RESERVATIONS

HOTEL RESERVATIONS & CANCELLATIONS: Whether or not you opt to secure reservations in advance depends on how flexible you want to be, how tight your schedule is, during which season you are traveling, and how disappointed you would be if your first choice were unavailable. Reservations are confining and usually must be guaranteed by a deposit. Refunds are difficult should you change your plans—especially at the last minute. Although reservations can be restrictive, it is nice not to spend a part of your vacation day searching for available accommodation, particularly during the peak summer months and holiday periods, and since many of the hotels in this guide are in remote areas it would be frustrating to arrive after hours of driving to find the only inn already full. Also, hotel space in the major cities is usually very scarce—even in the "off season" city hotels are frequently booked solid.

Should you decide to make reservations in advance, several options are discussed below. However, in each case, when making a reservation be sure to state clearly and exactly what you want, how many people are in your party, how many rooms you require, the category of room you prefer (standard, superior, deluxe), and your date of arrival and departure. Be sure to **spell out the month** since Europeans reverse the American numerical month/day order—to them 9/6 means June 9th, not September 6th as in the USA. Inquire about rates—which might have changed from those given in the book—and deposit requirements. It is also wise to advise them of your anticipated arrival time; discuss dining options if so desired; and ask for a confirmation letter with brochure and map to be sent to you.

The hotels appreciate your visit, value their inclusion in our guide, and frequently tell us they will take special care of our readers Many offer special rates to Karen Brown members (visit our website at *www.karenbrown.com.*) We hear over and over again from hotel owners that the people who use our guides are wonderful guests!

E-MAIL: This is our preferred way of making a reservation. All properties featured on the Karen Brown website that also have e-mail addresses have those addresses listed on their web pages (this information is constantly kept updated and correct). You can link directly to a property from its page on our website using its e-mail hyperlink. (See comments about dates above.)

FAX: Faxing is a very quick way to reach a hotel. If the hotel has a fax, we have included the number in its listing. As you are communicating with a machine, you also don't have to concern yourself with the time of day or worry about disturbing someone's sleep.

LETTER: If you have ample time before your departure, a letter is an inexpensive, though less efficient, way to request hotel space. Allow four weeks for a reply.

TELEPHONE: A call to the hotel is a very satisfactory way to make a reservation. You can immediately find out if space is available and, if not, make an alternative choice. For each hotel we have given the telephone number, including the area code. The best chance of finding the owner or manager who speaks English is to call when it is late afternoon in

Introduction–About Hotels

Switzerland (Switzerland is six hours ahead of New York). From the United States you dial 011 (the international code), then 41 (Switzerland's country code), then the city code (dropping the zero), and then the local telephone number. (Note: The zero before the city code is dropped only if calling from the United States—it must be included when dialing within Europe.)

WEBSITE

Please supplement this book by looking at the information provided on our Karen Brown website (*www.karenbrown.com*), which serves as an added dimension to our guides. Most of our favorite hotels are featured on the site (web participation is an hotel's choice) and on their web page you can usually link to their own website for even more detailed information and directions and also to their e-mail so that making a reservation is a breeze. Also featured on our site are comments, feedback, and discoveries from you, our readers; information on our latest finds; post-press updates; contest drawings for free books; special offers; unique features such as recipes and favorite destinations; and special savings offered by certain properties.

WHEELCHAIR ACCESSIBILITY

If an inn has *at least* one guestroom that is accessible by wheelchair, it is noted with the symbol ♿. This is not the same as saying it meets full disability standards. In reality it can be anything from a basic ground-floor room to a fully equipped facility. Please discuss your requirements when you call your chosen place to stay to determine if they have accommodation that suits your needs and preference.

Introduction–About Hotels

Sightseeing Reference

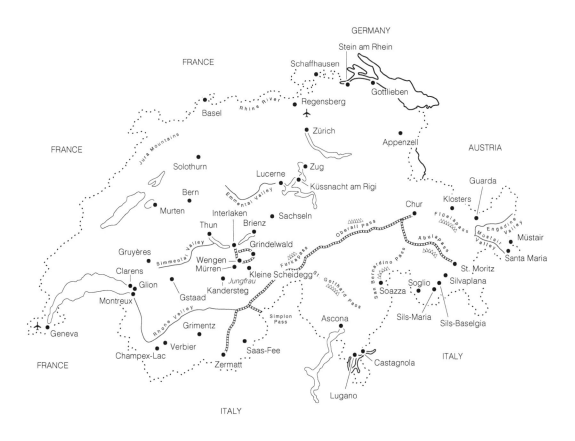

GERMANY

FRANCE

Stein am Rhein

Schaffhausen

Gottlieben

Regensberg

Rhine River

Basel

Zürich

FRANCE

Appenzell

AUSTRIA

Jura Mountains

Solothurn

Lucerne

Zug

Küssnacht am Rigi

Guarda

Bern

Emmental Valley

Klosters

Chur

Flüelapass

Engadine Valley

Müstair

Murten

Interlaken

Sachseln

Oberalp Pass

Abulapass

Müstair Valley

Thun

Brienz

Santa Maria

Grindelwald

Furkapass

St. Moritz

Gruyères

Simmental Valley

Wengen

Kleine Scheidegg

St. Gotthard Pass

San Bernardino Pass

Silvaplana

Clarens

Mürren

Soglio

Glion

Jungfrau

Kandersteg

Soazza

Sils-Maria

Sils-Baselgia

Montreux

Gstaad

Simplon Pass

Ascona

Geneva

Grimentz

ITALY

FRANCE

Verbier

Champex-Lac

Saas-Fee

Castagnola

Zermatt

Lugano

ITALY

33

Sightseeing Reference

The five suggested itineraries in this guide crisscross back and forth across Switzerland describing routes tailored for individual whims and budgets. Because certain key towns reappear in several itineraries, we decided to have an individual sightseeing section as a quick reference of what to expect along your route. The following towns, listed alphabetically, appear in the itineraries as sightseeing and, in most cases, overnight destinations.

APPENZELL

Appenzell is a picture-book village, popular with tourists who flock to see the fanciful paintings on the façades of the buildings, a colorful variety of artwork—landscapes, folk art, flowers, abstract designs, animals, and people. Appenzell is famous also for exquisite embroidery and delicious cheeses. Politically, it is well known for its demonstration of real democracy: on the last Sunday in April, the citizens, usually wearing their colorful traditional costumes, gather in the village square to elect representatives to their local canton with a show of hands.

Another appealing aspect of Appenzell is the tranquil countryside that surrounds it. This area of Switzerland is lush with rolling, gentle green fields dotted with plump, happy cows lazily munching grass to the rhythm of their cow bells. Snuggled in these lovely pastures are large farmhouses adorned with masses of flowers, the family home attached to the barn so that the animals are easily accessible during winter snows.

ASCONA

In days gone by Ascona was a sleepy fishing village, but today tourists are its main source of activity and it is no wonder—Ascona abounds with character. The lake laps at the dock where boats are moored next to the colorful central square, which is framed by Italian-looking pastel-colored buildings with heavy tiled roofs. Behind the front row of houses, tiny lanes spider-web into the medieval village. From Ascona, steamers ply Lake Maggiore, one of Switzerland's most romantic lakes. When the weather is cold and dreary in the north, it is a tempting option to head to the Swiss-Italian Lake District where the sun shines most of the year and flowers bloom all winter.

BASEL

The town of Basel is well worth a visit. It is an industrial city, the second largest in Switzerland, and the outskirts are not very attractive, but when you arrive at the heart of the old town, you find a delightful medieval city—a very real city functioning as a center for banking, insurance, trade, and commerce. At the border of France and Germany and linked by the River Rhine to central Europe, Basel has a very important strategic location. The Rhine acts as the gateway to the North Sea, so Basel is a very busy port.

The splendidly preserved old town is a delight to stroll around. Here you discover, tucked away on back streets, charming squares adorned with joyful little fountains. Be sure to visit the 12th-century cathedral and the market square (*Marktplatz*), which is host every morning to a flower and vegetable market. The town hall (*Rathaus*) dates from the 16th century and is beautifully decorated with frescos. There is an excellent Museum of Fine Arts (*Kunstmuseum)* displaying works of art of the 15th and 16th centuries. The Museum of Antique Art (*Antikenmuseum*) features sculptures and art dating from pre-Hellenic times.

In summer there are boat tours that offer a leisurely view of the city. This method of sightseeing is especially interesting because from the river you can view many of the marvelous old buildings that line it and also cross under some of the bridges that span the River Rhine so colorfully.

BERN

Bern is an enticingly well-preserved 16th-century walled city, perched on a plateau almost made into an island by a loop of the River Aare. Further enhancing the picture, the mountains rise in the background. The setting alone would make Bern worth a stop, but the town itself has lots of character and interesting sightseeing attractions.

Marktgasse, the main street of the old part of Bern, has charming medieval buildings, arcaded sidewalks, intriguing shops, and whimsical fountains. However, my favorite attraction in Bern is the clock tower, the town's West Gate until the 13th century, which appeals to the child in all of us. Four minutes before the hour the "show" begins: as the bell peals, a succession of figures parade across the clock including the most popular of all—darling little bear cubs. Bern is an easy walking city. Just a stroll from the clock tower is the Nydegg Bridge from where you have wonderful views of the town and, if you are a photographer, some great shots.

BRIENZ & BALLENBERG

Nestled on the shores of Lake Brienz, Brienz is a picturesque town overlooking the Giessbach Falls and the surrounding Alpine peaks. This is a famous wood-carving center and most of the carvings available for purchase throughout Switzerland come from this lakeside town. It is a charming town and its web of old narrow streets shadowed by dark wooden chalet-style houses and shops is fun to explore.

For a breathtaking, panoramic view of the Bernese Alps and Lake Brienz, consider a journey on the Brienz Rothorn Bahn. This wonderful old steam locomotive traverses some exceptionally beautiful scenery on its three-hour ascent by rack-and-pinion railway to the summit of the Rothorn (2,350 meters). There is a hotel at the summit, both commercial and functional in decor and comfort, where you can dine or overnight, the Hotel Restaurant Rothorn Kulm, tel: (033) 951 12 21, fax: (033) 951 12 51. For additional information about the train and schedules, contact Brienz Rothorn Bahn, tel: (033) 952 22 22, e-mail: info@brienz-rothorn-bahn.ch, web at *www.brienz-rothorn-bahn.ch*.

Located on the outskirts of Brienz, by the Wyssensee, Ballenberg is a marvelous open-air museum that serves as a wonderful introduction to the regional architecture and cultures of Switzerland. More than 70 historical buildings from the various cantons have been relocated to this park of some 80 hectares. You can tour the park on foot or, for a fee, by horse and buggy. The museum buildings, from a half-timbered Bernese chalet to a thatched farmhouse from the Aargau, are all authentically furnished and surrounded by a lush landscape of gardens, meadows, and fields of grain.

Ballenberg Open-Air Museum

People dressed in costume work the museum, bringing back a vision of centuries past. You can observe crafts such as basket weaving, purchase a picnic bounty of bread from the baker and sausage or cheese from the farmer, or settle in at the village inn for a meal. Due to the vastness of the park, even if you selectively visit just a few cantons, plan on allocating at least a half day to visit Ballenberg—however, you could easily spend up to two full days here. The museum is open April 15 to October 31, from 10 am to 5 pm. The museum has two entrances: Ballenberg-East is most convenient from Lucerne and Ballenberg-West is recommended from Bern and Interlaken. You can arrange for a guided tour by contacting the museum in advance: Swiss Open-Air Museum Ballenberg, CH-3855

Brienz, Switzerland, tel: (033) 952 10 30, fax: (033) 952 10 39, e-mail: info@ballenberg.ch, web: *www.ballenberg.ch*.

CASTAGNOLA & GANDRIA

Castagnola is a lakeside community close to Lugano. From Castagnola there is a scenic walking path connecting Castagnola with the small town of Gandria. This trail hugs the shore of Lake Lugano and makes a pleasant walk and you can stop along the way at one of the little lakefront cafés for refreshment. Castagnola is famous for the Villa Favorita, which is perched on the hillside above the lake. Housing a very impressive private art collection, the Villa Favorita is a 17th-century mansion surrounded by beautifully landscaped gardens, with magnificent views of Lugano.

CHAMPEX-LAC

Champex-Lac is a small town on the shores of a high-mountain lake 75 kilometers south of Montreux. The Mont Blanc massif rises beyond the lake, reflecting in its still waters. In summer this resort is especially appealing for families who enjoy boating, hiking, bicycling, swimming, and horseback riding.

CHUR

Chur, though not well known as a tourist destination, is the most important city in eastern Switzerland. In addition to being a modern commercial center, Chur has an attractive walled, medieval section with narrow, winding streets (many open only for foot traffic), quaint cobbled alleys, charming little squares graced by fountains, and colorful buildings dating back to the 15th century. There are pretty shops and many good restaurants. Green hills form a backdrop to the town while the majestic mountains can be seen in the distance. Chur is on the main rail route, making it a convenient starting point for train travel.

CLARENS

Clarens is a jewel on the shores of Lake Geneva, a discreet tree-sheltered oasis between Montreux and Vevey. The glorious setting and panoramic views across the lake to the snow-clad French Alps have attracted wealthy visitors from all over the world—many of whom stayed to build beautiful villas.

GENEVA

Geneva is frequently thought of as a modern city—a city of banking and commerce; an international city housing the Palais des Nations; a city of beautiful shops; a city of museums and culture; an industrial city. All this is true, but Geneva also has one of the most attractive medieval sections in Switzerland, "Old Geneva," located on the south side of the River Rhône. Here the hills rise steeply from the shore of the lake and the streets twist and turn in a maze of fascinating little shops, fountains, flower-filled squares, and charming buildings. This area is crowned by the 12th-century Saint Peter's Cathedral, which dominates the old town. Within the church you find a triangular chair supposedly used by Calvin and the tomb of the Duc de Rohn who was the leader of the French Protestants during the time of Henry IV. Perhaps the most spectacular feature of Saint Peter's is the climb to the top of the north tower where you have a panoramic view of Geneva and beyond to the lake and the majestic backdrop of the Alps. While you are in the old town, you might also want to see the town hall, which dates from the 16th century. After visiting Saint Peter's, wander down the little twisting streets, exploring small antique shops and back alleys—you cannot get lost because it is all downhill and when you are at the bottom, you are at the lake. Along the banks of the lake there is a park with a clock made out of flowers.

On the north side of the Rhône circling around the lake is the newer section of Geneva. In this area there are lovely lake promenades punctuated with splendid flower gardens, stately hotels, small squares, and fancy shops. This, too, is a perfect strolling part of the city—especially in early spring when the tulips are beautiful. Within walking distance are many museums and interesting places to see. The Palais des Nations, located in the Park de l'Ariana, is open daily except special holidays but, like many museums, is closed for a few hours in the middle of the day. There are many guided tours. The palace was once the headquarters of the League of Nations and is now the seat of the European branch of the United Nations. The Petit Palais Museum, which features French painters from the end of the Impressionist period, is open daily except Monday mornings and holidays. The Museum of Old Musical Instruments displays a wonderful collection of European musical instruments. Since you are in Switzerland, the home of the clock, visit the Watch and Clock Museum with displays of timepieces from their origin to the present day.

You really cannot help being captivated by Geneva with its sophisticated beauty and international air. As you meander through the parks and promenades, you could be anywhere in the world—you see all nationalities and hear all languages. This is a city we all seem to love and share.

GLION

Glion is a small town perched in the hills high above Montreux. Because of its superb location, with a panorama of Lake Geneva and the mountains, Glion has attracted the wealthy, who have built beautiful mansions nestled among the trees. You can reach Glion by car or, if arriving from Geneva by boat, by a tram connecting the dock at Territet with Glion. There is also a train from Montreux to Glion.

GOTTLIEBEN

Gottlieben is located on the River Rhine just before it enters Lake Constance. This is a dear little village hugging the water's edge, with narrow, picturesque streets which are fun to explore. The town is of special interest because of the Hotel Krone, picturesquely situated on the banks of the river. Gottlieben serves as an excellent base from which to explore the region by water rather than by road. From Gottlieben you can take ferry boats down the Rhine to Stein am Rhein and Schaffhausen or you can travel by boat on to Lake Constance.

GRIMENTZ

Grimentz is a small, old-world farming village snuggled on a plateau at the end of the D'Anniviers Valley, which stretches south from the Rhône Valley. As with other charming Swiss towns, the government protects its architectural standards. This is a town of small Valais-style wooden houses darkened almost black with age, usually with slate roofs and suspended above the ground on stone pillars. My guess is that the Grimentz of old could never have been prettier than it is today when each resident seems to vie with his neighbor to grow the most outstanding flowers. The effect is sensational—brilliant blue sky, snow-capped mountains, green pastures, and antique homes exploding in geraniums.

GRINDELWALD

Grindelwald captures for many the romanticized image of Switzerland. It is a charming Alpine village sprawled on a lovely expanse of meadows and surrounded by magnificent towering mountains. It is a popular destination for exploring the Jungfrau Range for it is as close as you can come by car to view the spectacular giants of the Jungfrau region: the Eiger rising to 3,970 meters, the Wetterhorn to 3,701 meters, and the Mettenberg to 3,104 meters. From the little station in town the train departs for the dramatic Kleine Scheidegg and on to the Jungfraujoch. For further information, please refer to the Jungfraujoch sightseeing section later in the book.

Grindelwald is a draw for sport enthusiasts year round. In winter the focus is on the snow conditions, terrain, and the best adventures in downhill and cross-country skiing. In summer the same lifts that take skiers up the mountain give hikers a head start along trails that climb in the shadow of the Eiger. There are also trams that operate only in summer and make hikes to glaciers and high meadows feasible in the span of a day.

GRUYÈRES

Gruyères is a beautiful little medieval village hugging the crest of a miniature mountain just north of Lake Geneva and south of Bern. This is such a unique and charming little village that it is considered a national monument and its architectural purity is protected by the Swiss government. Climb its cobbled streets to the castle that crowns it. Perhaps your visit will coincide with a day when horn blowers dressed in traditional costume sound off on the village square—it is enchanting. Cars are not allowed into the village but there are several parking lots strategically located on the road that winds up to the town.

Another bonus for Gruyères, as you probably guessed from the name of the town, is its location in the center of one of Switzerland's famous dairy areas—the cheeses and creams are marvelous. Stop for a famous Gruyères quiche, linger over a crock of rich fondue, or, if in season, delicious fresh berries and thick cream.

Gruyères is a convenient town to use as a headquarters for a few days. The countryside in summer is exactly what you dream about as being truly Switzerland: the meadows are incredibly green, contented cows with tinkling bells graze lazily in the pastures, wildflowers abound in the fields, and windowboxes full of bright geraniums adorn the houses, all enhanced by the backdrop of gorgeous mountains. One short excursion takes you to the small museum-factory just at the bottom of the hill as you drive down from the town. In this modern factory you see how cheeses are made in the various cantons in Switzerland and also watch a movie explaining the process, narrated in English. Also, if you are a cheese enthusiast, you can make short excursions to visit some of the other little villages in the area and sample their dairy products—you might come home a little plumper, but a connoisseur of the delicious Swiss cheese.

The secret to discovering the enchantment of Gruyères is to spend the night here so that the town is yours in the hushed morning and the still hours of dusk. Leave at midday when the tour buses deposit their eager load of tourists and return late in the day, to sit on the terrace and have a drink, listening to the tinkling of cow bells as the sun fades.

GSTAAD

In spite of the fact that Gstaad has an international reputation as a very chic ski resort catering to the wealthy jet set, the town retains much of its old-world, small-town, charming simplicity. The setting of Gstaad is magnificent, with rugged mountain peaks rising steeply on each side of the valley. In summer the hiking and mountain climbing is excellent, while in winter Gstaad offers one of the most famous networks of ski trails in Switzerland. The center of town is pedestrian-only, which makes it even more attractive.

GUARDA, SENT & TARASP CASTLE

Guarda has a spectacular location high on a mountain shelf overlooking the Engadine Valley. The main recreation here is simply being out of doors exploring the beckoning mountain paths and soaking up the sensational beauty of the mountain peaks. However, there is some "formal" sightseeing that can be included in your plans. Nearby is the extremely picturesque Tarasp Castle, which crowns a tiny mountain across the valley from Guarda. There are guided tours of the castle during the summer months. Also near Guarda is the tiny town of Sent which, like Guarda, is famous for its many old houses covered with intricate designs. Sent also has a scenic setting overlooking the valley.

INTERLAKEN

Interlaken, which translates to "between the lakes," has a fabulous location on a spit of land connecting Lake Brienz and Lake Thun. This position makes it a prime destination for those who want to take the circle train excursion to enjoy the majestic summit of the Jungfraujoch. (Please refer to Jungfraujoch sightseeing which follows.) There are also numerous steamers that in season depart from Interlaken and ply the waters of Lake Brienz and Lake Thun. Interlaken has many grand Victorian-style hotels and  fancy shops, restaurants, and the allure of its casino. For many years it has attracted tourists from all over the world who come to enjoy the unbeatable combination of two of the most beautiful lakes in Switzerland and glorious mountain peaks.

JUNGFRAUJOCH EXCURSION

The Jungfraujoch excursion is a journey on a series of small trains, synchronized to provide you with a perfect prize—the Jungfraujoch, with the highest train station in Europe sitting 92 meters below the summit of the Jungfrau. The most popular starting points for this outing are any of the following train stations: Interlaken Ost, Lauterbrunnen, Grindelwald, or Wengen. Although the trip can be taken in segments, or as a side trip from one of the starting points, most tourists prefer to squeeze the ultimate enjoyment from their outing by taking the complete circle trip from Interlaken.

The Jungfraujoch excursion is one of the highlights of Switzerland, and one that is mentioned in four of the following itineraries. Unless you have traveled the route, it sounds quite complicated, but it is not. We explain, step by step, how this fabulous mountain adventure is put together and then you can tailor the trip to suit your special needs, beginning and ending at the town you have chosen to spend the night. The diagram on the following page demonstrates how the journey and options coordinate.

The complete circle trip begins at Interlaken Ost (Interlaken East) train station. However, you can also climb aboard at any of the stations, for example, Lauterbrunnen, Kleine Scheidegg, Wengen, or Grindelwald, and the fare adjusts accordingly. Assuming Interlaken as your departure point, it is a 25-minute train ride to Lauterbrunnen where you change trains for the 45-minute ride up the mountain to Kleine Scheidegg (stopping en route to pick up passengers at the little town of Wengen). You have to change trains again at Kleine Scheidegg for the final ascent of the Jungfraujoch excursion to the base of the Jungfrau. The last leg of your train adventure is an incredible 55 minutes in which the train creeps up the steep mountain and disappears into a 6½-kilometer tunnel — reappearing at the Jungfraubahn, the highest rail station in Europe. It is possible to take an elevator even higher through the mountain to a vista point from where, on a clear day, it seems you can see the whole of Switzerland. You also find an ice palace carved into the glacier, dog-sled rides, shops, a post office, restaurants, etc. For this journey, be sure to take sturdy shoes for walking on the glacier, gloves, a warm sweater or jacket, sunscreen, and sunglasses. When you leave the Jungfraujoch, it is necessary to retrace your journey to Kleine Scheidegg. For scenic variety, many prefer to return to Interlaken from Kleine Scheidegg by a circle route. To do this, board the train for Grindelwald where you connect with another train that takes you directly to Interlaken.

The Jungfraujoch is a very expensive excursion, but a once-in-a-lifetime adventure, especially when the weather cooperates and blue skies color a magnificent backdrop for these majestic peaks. There are numerous daily train departures and tickets are available for purchase at hotels, campsites, tourist offices, train stations, or travel agencies. A bargain for early risers is the "Good Morning Ticket," which offers a 40% discount. This is available May 1–October 31 on the first regular morning train with a return departure at 12 noon at the latest and November 1–April 30 on the first or second regular morning train with return at any time.

Jungfraujoch Excursion

Lake Thun

Lake Brienz

Interlaken
Ost Station

Train ▭▭▭▭
Car ───
Cablecar ┝┿┿┿┥

Zweilütschinen

Grindelwald

Wengen

Lauterbrunnen

Kleine
Scheidegg

Mürren ●┿┿┿┿┥

Stechelberg

Jungfraujoch

KANDERSTEG

Kandersteg is a hamlet nestled at the end of the Kandertal Valley. The road ends here so those who want to continue on across the mountain range for the shortcut to the Rhône Valley must travel by train. (If you are driving, it is at Kandersteg that you put your car on the train for the piggy-back ride through the mountain.) However, Kandersteg is far more than a train depot—this is a lovely little mountain village with a stupendous backdrop of majestic mountains, a paradise for mountain lovers.

KLEINE SCHEIDEGG

Kleine Scheidegg is the jumping-off point for the final leg of the Jungfraujoch excursion (see earlier description for details on this outing). Located above the timberline, the town is actually just a cluster of buildings hugging the windswept plateau. The wide, sweeping vistas of the rugged peaks of the Eiger, the Mönch, and the Jungfrau are overpowering. If the day is sunny, it is great fun to sit out on the open terrace with a beer and a bratwurst while soaking in the splendor of the mountains and watching tourists set off on the tiny train that soon disappears as it tunnels into the glacier.

KLOSTERS

The town of Klosters backs up to the same mountains as Davos and actually the two ski areas interconnect like a giant spider web. Although much of Klosters is newly constructed in response to the need for tourist accommodation, the town has grown with a gracious style encompassing the Swiss chalet motif. There are many lovely shops and restaurants. The town is very well situated for hiking in the summer or skiing in the winter. The train station is the terminus for a cable lift that rises high above the village to the marvelous ski runs. Also popular in winter are tobogganing, cross-country skiing, curling, and ice skating. However, my favorite time for Klosters is the summer when the fields are vibrant with wildflowers, with the majestic mountains standing guard.

KÜSSNACHT AM RIGI

Sometimes there is confusion about the location of Küssnacht am Rigi because there is a town with a very similar name—Küsnacht—located on Lake Zürich. However, Küssnacht am Rigi is a charming little village with some colorful medieval buildings on the northern tip of a small finger of Lake Lucerne. Since there is ferry service from Lucerne, Küssnacht am Rigi is popular for a day's excursion or an overnight stay. Küssnacht am Rigi is also associated with the folk hero William Tell who, at a site nearby, is said to have shot the Austrian governor with his mighty crossbow while leading his people in their battle to win freedom from Hapsburg rule.

LUCERNE

There is not a wealth of tourist attractions in Lucerne—the attraction is the city itself. Lucerne is brimming with tourists, but you certainly understand its popularity when you wander the charming little streets filled with colorful shops or stroll the river promenade stopping for a snack in one of the quaint cafés set out on the banks of the River Reuss. It is enjoyable to cross the multitude of bridges that span the river and meander along the shore of Lake Lucerne. Another excursion is to board one of the steamers for a lazy journey around the lake. Yes, tourists have found Lucerne, but it is so lovely, I do not think you will mind sharing it with others. Also in Lucerne is the Museum of Transport and Communications, one of Switzerland's finest museums. This display follows the development of transportation and communication up to the exploration of space. Children are especially enthralled with this wonderful museum.

Recommended for a sunny day is an outing from Lucerne to the highest mountain peak in the area, Mount Pilatus. The most enjoyable route for this excursion is to take the lake steamer to the town of Alpnachstad and then the electric cog railway up to the top of the mountain. From the rail terminal it is only about a ten-minute walk to the peak of the mountain where there is a spectacular panorama.

Another excursion from Lucerne is to the town of Einsiedeln to see the home of the famous Black Madonna. The monastery of Einsiedeln was founded by Meinrad, a Benedictine monk, who built a small chapel for the Black Madonna (a statue of the Virgin Mary), which had been given to him by Zürich priests. Meinrad was later murdered by some men who mistakenly thought he had hidden treasures. Later, the Monastery of Einsiedeln was built over Meinrad's grave and another chapel was erected to house the Black Madonna. This site has become a pilgrimage, not only for Catholics, but for tourists who are attracted to the Einsiedeln Abbey, an excellent example of baroque architecture.

LUGANO

Lugano is an appealing medieval town hugging the northern shore of Lake Lugano. In Lugano there are several "musts." First, you will love exploring the old city. This is best done by walking, since many of the streets are closed to cars. Be sure to visit the Cathedral of Saint Lawrence (San Lorenzo), famous for its elegant Renaissance façade and lovely fresco decoration. Another "must" for Lugano is to take advantage of the steamers that ply the lake from its dock. You can stretch your boat ride out to an all-day excursion or squeeze it into a couple of hours. My recommendation would be to go to Morcote, a charming little village rising from the shores of the lake. If possible, allow enough time in Morcote to have lunch at the Hotel Carina-Carlton's cheerful café, which juts out over the water. If you feel industrious, you can climb up the steep back alleys which will bring you to the Church of Santa Maria del Sasso, which contains some outstanding 16th-century frescos. Also in Morcote there is a delightful private park where you will find beautiful plants artistically displayed in gardens overlooking the lake. The park is only a few minutes' walk from the Hotel Carina-Carlton. Another fun boat trip from Lugano is to Gandria, another village clinging to the lakeside filled with flowers and surrounded by vineyards. Both Gandria and Morcote are photographers' dreams.

MONTREUX & THE CASTLE OF CHILLON

Montreux is a sophisticated town nestled along the shore of the eastern tip of Lake Geneva (also called Lac Léman). A beautiful, densely wooded hill rises steeply to the east, forming a protective screen behind the town and capturing the sun. Montreux's view out over the gorgeous blue waters of the lake, which is rimmed to the south with soaring mountains, is breathtaking. An old-fashioned promenade traces the waterfront, a favorite spot for a lazy stroll. Because of its allure as a place to live, large apartments have been built in Montreux, but there remains an old-world ambiance to the town, which still has many super-deluxe hotels and exclusive mansions with lawns stretching to the water's edge. Artists and musicians too have long been drawn to the beauty of Montreux. For those who enjoy gambling, Montreux has a casino, but one of the main attractions is the romantic Castle of Chillon, perched on a tiny peninsula 3 kilometers south of town.

MÜRREN

Mürren is a village clinging to a ledge high above the Lauterbrunnen Valley, with a startlingly steep granite wall dropping straight down from the village to the valley far below. The only access is by cable car from Stechelberg, tram from Lauterbrunnen, or, of course, for the true outdoorsman, by foot. Across the valley, the Jungfrau towers into the sky, incredibly close, incredibly powerful. The Jungfrau circle of towns (Grindelwald, Wengen, and Kleine Scheidegg) is on the opposite side of the valley. (See the earlier description of the Jungfraujoch excursion.) If you don't have time for the Jungfraujoch excursion, there is a thrilling mountain adventure right from Mürren. Just step again onto the cable car, which will whisk you ever upward (with a change from one cable car to another en route) and get off at the icy barrens at the top of the mountain, the Schilthorn. Here you are treated to an awesome view of some of the most incredible mountain peaks in the world, right at your fingertips. Plan to have lunch here. There is a dramatic revolving restaurant with walls of glass called the Piz Gloria, which slowly circles so that you can savor the view while you dine.

MURTEN

Murten is a sensational walled medieval village nestled on the banks of Lake Murten— only a short distance from Bern or Neuchâtel. You enter Murten through a gate in the medieval wall that completely surrounds this fairy-tale village with flowerboxes everywhere and brightly painted fountains accenting tiny squares. The entire effect is one of festivity. Before exploring the town, you might want first to climb to the ramparts and walk the walls for a bird's-eye view of what you are going to see. Murten is like an outdoor museum. Strolling through the town, you can study many of the 15th-century buildings and the walls that date from the 12th century. There is a castle at the western end of town built by Peter of Savoy in the 13th century. As you walk along, watch for the town hall, the French church, the German church, the Bern Gate (with one of the oldest clock towers in Switzerland), and the Historical Museum, which displays weapons, banners, and uniforms from the Burgundian battles.

MÜSTAIR

Müstair is a simple village at the eastern end of the Müstair Valley, just before the Italian border. This is a pretty little village of thick-walled houses dating back to the 13th century whose character seems more Italian than Swiss—it's as if the border line has slipped back to the favor of Italy. Very few people speak English here——the ambiance is one of an authentic old European town, untouched by commercialism. The dialect is decidedly Italian and the locals' salutation is *arrevoir*.

REGENSBERG

Regensberg is very, very special. Here, only a few kilometers north of Zürich, and about 20 minutes from the Zürich airport, is a perfectly preserved medieval village topping a vineyard-laced knoll. Regensberg makes an ideal base for your arrival into Switzerland or a wonderful choice for a few days to relax before heading home. It is one of the prettiest tiny villages in Switzerland.

SAAS FEE

Saas Fee is a delightful town located at the end of the Saastal or Saas Valley, which branches off from the road to the much more famous resort of Zermatt. Ringed by more than a dozen mountains, the town occupies a terrace high above the valley. Accessible only by bus and car, the town is closed to traffic—all cars must be left in the huge multi-story car park on the edge of town. Park in parking lot 1 and if you are staying overnight.

By the time you have unloaded, dialed your hotel, and parked your car, the hotel's electric cart will be there to pick you up.

Saas Fee is primarily a ski town but is still bustling in summer with hikers and tourists. There are attractive shops (lots of watches and skiing and hiking equipment) and some delightful restaurants. Hiking opportunities abound, from gentle walks to "high routes," challenging hikes in the mountains.

Saas Fee offers some intriguing diversions, including rides on the underground Metro to the Mittelallalin, site of the world's highest revolving restaurant. Even more fascinating is the Ice Pavilion, the world's largest ice cavern, where the exhibits include a crevasse within the Fee Glacier. If you are staying for several days, consider purchasing the seven-day Wander Pass which covers fees for the Ice Pavilion, a day of skiing, Saas-Fee museums, buses, and cable cars along the Saas Valley.

SACHSELN

Sachseln, a small town on the road from Lucerne to Interlaken, has great religious significance for Catholics who come in great numbers to pray to Saint Nicholas of Flüe, a peasant who, in the 15th century, is credited with saving the confederacy. Saint Nicholas, the father of ten children, was a deeply religious man who, in his 50s, felt the irresistible call to live the life of solitude (with ten children, perhaps it is understandable!), so he went up into the hills behind Sachseln where he spent his life in meditation. Because of his reputation as a man of inspired wisdom, leaders came to him for advice and he is credited with negotiating a peaceful compromise between the cantons when conflict seemed inevitable in 1481.

SAINT MORITZ

Known to the jet-set elite throughout the world as *the* place to be seen in the ski season, Saint Moritz is also popular as a summer resort. The town backs right up to the mountain so it is just a short walk to the funicular to go skiing. From its terraced position on the side of the hill, Saint Moritz looks down to a pretty tree-rimmed lake. In winter horse races cross the frozen expanse and in summer a path skirts its edge. In town, the streets are lined with chic boutiques selling exquisite merchandise and in the center of this shopping paradise is the famous Palace Hotel, very lovely, very expensive. If you want to rub elbows with the rich and famous, this is where you should be. However, in the hotel description section of this guide you find our recommendations of some very pleasant, less expensive hotels. Saint Moritz has not grown with the same purity of architecture as some other ski areas such as Gstaad and Zermatt, but it is much less "concrete high-rise" than its sister ski area, Davos. If you are a movie buff, climb the steep mountain trail to see the cabin that was used in the original *Heidi* movie.

SANTA MARIA

Santa Maria is a small hamlet intersected by the road that travels through the beautiful Müstair Valley. There are many lovely old Grisons-style buildings in the town and a very attractive church. Nearby is the Swiss National Park, an oasis for wildlife and vegetation. The park is very popular with Swiss families who come here to hike.

SCHAFFHAUSEN

Schaffhausen is a quaint medieval city that grew up along the banks of the Rhine just above the point where the river plummets to a lower level, forming the Rheinfall, one of Europe's most spectacular waterfalls. Boats cannot, of course, navigate the rushing waters, and in days gone by, their cargo was carried around the falls. Schaffhausen grew up to accommodate this trader traffic. Within Schaffhausen there are many characterful houses, real architectural gems—many with oriel windows adding colorful detail. There are also several fountains, old towers, and, of course, a castle perched on the hill above the town. While in Schaffhausen you will want to make the very short excursion to see the Rheinfall. Sightseeing boats take you to the base of the falls.

SILS-BASELGIA, SILS-MARIA & SILVAPLANA

Approximately 10 kilometers south of the famous resort of Saint Moritz are the "sister" villages of Sils-Baselgia and Sils-Maria, located on a thread of land connecting the two tiny lakes of Silvaplana and Silser. The Sils area is a paradise for cross-country skiing in the winter and hiking, boating, fishing, sail-surfing, and swimming in the summer. Silvaplana, located about 6 kilometers south of Saint Moritz, is much less commercial than its next-door neighbor, but is still a bustling summer and winter resort.

SOAZZA

Although not as well known as some of Switzerland's other jewels, Soazza stands out as one of its most picturesque mountain villages. This tiny hamlet (with only about 300 inhabitants) is perched on a sunny terrace overlooking the gentle, verdant Mesocco Valley, which leads north from Bellinzona to the 2,063-meter-high San Bernardino Pass, a route that has possibly been used since prehistoric times. This picture-perfect village is further enhanced by a lovely 13th-century church perched atop a knoll overlooking the town. The handsome stone houses that line the narrow, cobbled streets seem untouched by time. The fact that Soazza is secreted off the main highway has helped preserve its pristine beauty.

SOGLIO

The mountain setting of the little town of Soglio is one of the most dramatically beautiful in all of Switzerland. Soglio is perched on a ledge high above the beautiful Bregaglia Valley, looking across to some of the most impressive mountain peaks in Switzerland. The town is tiny—no more than a few narrow alley-like streets lined with wonderful old houses. The church with its high spire soaring into the sky completes the picture-book setting perfectly. Soglio is not only a picturesque stopover, but in addition is a wonderful center for walking, with beautiful paths along the ledge of the mountain. Chestnut trees line some of these beautiful trails and although you are high above the valley, the walking is easy.

SOLOTHURN

The town of Solothurn, one of the oldest Roman settlements in Switzerland, is a completely walled medieval city built along the shore of the River Aare. A modern industrial city has grown up around Solothurn, but once you cross through the gate, like magic you are transported back hundreds of years. This pretty medieval town has remained unspoiled. You are greeted by colorfully painted fountains, charming little squares, beautifully preserved buildings, the famous Saint Ursen Cathedral, wrought-iron signs, and houses with brightly painted shutters.

STEIN AM RHEIN

The walled town of Stein am Rhein, built along the banks of the River Rhine, is one of the most photogenic towns in Switzerland. After entering the main gates, you find yourself in a fairy-tale town with each building almost totally covered with fanciful paintings. The town is very small so it will not take long to explore, but it is certainly worth a visit. If you are taking a ferry along the river, Stein am Rhein makes a super stopover for lunch or a fun place to spend the night after the tour buses depart.

Garden lovers will not want to miss taking the boat excursion to the tiny island of Mainau just across the German border. Lovely, fragrant gardens bloom from March to October in the grounds of an 18th-century castle owned by a Swedish count.

WENGEN

Part of the charm of Wengen is that it can be reached only by train. You leave your car in the parking lot at the Lauterbrunnen station and take the train for the spectacular 20-minute ride up the mountain. As the train pulls up the steep incline, you catch glimpses through the lacy trees of the magnificent valley below. When you reach Wengen, you will be entranced: it has one of the most glorious sites in the world—high on a mountain plateau overlooking the breathtaking Lauterbrunnen Valley, a valley enclosed with walls of granite traced with cascading waterfalls. A backdrop for the total picture is the awe-inspiring Jungfrau massif with its three famous peaks, the Jungfrau, the Mönch, and the Eiger. This is a center for outdoor enthusiasts and sportsmen, while tourists come from all over the world to soak up the spectacular Alpine beauty. Summer is my favorite time of year in Wengen when the marvelous walking paths beckon. Along these trails there are new vistas at every turn, each more beautiful than the last. If walking is too gentle for your spirit, you can take climbs into the Bernese Oberland. If you are going to do some serious climbing, you should hire a local guide to accompany you. In addition to being a mecca for the mountain enthusiast, Wengen is also an excellent base for the excursion to the Jungfrau (please refer to the Jungfraujoch section).

ZERMATT

Cars are not allowed in Zermatt, so leave your car beside the Täsch railway station and ride the train in. As you arrive at the station, you will notice many electric carts and horse-drawn carriages owned by the hotels for shuttling guests to and from the station. If your hotel's cart is not there, locate your hotel on the large board in the train station, dial the code of your hotel and advise them of your arrival. They'll pick you up free of charge.

Zermatt is a city in the sky, not the sleepy little mountain village of yesterday. It takes patience to uncover the remnants of the "Old Zermatt"—the weathered wooden chalets weighted beneath heavy slate roofs—but they are still there hidden on little side alleys and dotted in the mountain meadows.

Although there are now shopping arcades, numerous hotels, condominiums springing up in the meadows, and tourists packing the streets, Zermatt is still one of our favorite places in Switzerland—for some things never change: the Matterhorn, rising in majestic splendor as a backdrop to the town, is still one of the most dramatic sights in the world. (Do not miss sunrise over the Matterhorn. Just as the sun comes up, the tip of the Matterhorn is enveloped in a pinkish-orange glow, which grows larger until it encompasses the whole mountain.) As you leave the center of Zermatt, within a few minutes you are again in the "Zermatt of old," with gigantic mountain peaks piercing the sky. It is so beautiful that it's frustrating—each path is beckoning "try me"—you want to go in every direction at once.

The great influx of tourists definitely has advantages too: fun little shops filled with tempting wares line the streets; cozy restaurants make each meal decision a dilemma; new hotels have opened, giving the traveler a great selection of accommodation. The pride of making Zermatt worthy of its reputation has stimulated competition among the hoteliers and shopkeepers—each appears to strive to make his flowerbox more gorgeous than his neighbor's, resulting in a profusion of color.

Two popular sightseeing excursions are the Gornegrat and Klein Matterhorn, neither of which should be taken if visibility is poor. The Gornegrat ascent entails a ride on a cog railway up to the Gornegrat Station, which is located on a rocky ridge looking over the town of Zermatt and beyond to the Matterhorn. From the Gornegrat Station a walk down to the next station gives you views of the Matterhorn and the surrounding mountains. The Klein Matterhorn ascent involves a ride on a small cable car to a mid-station, then three or four rides on a large gondola/cable car. The station at the summit is at the highest altitude of any station in Europe (3,820 meters). The views are spectacular.

There are numerous well marked footpaths and walks. You can follow one of the beautifully marked trails drifting out from the village core or take a chair lift, tram, or train up the mountain, from which point you can walk all or part of the way down. The number of tourists also justifies numerous small cafés scattered along the trails. It is truly the way to hike when you can stop along the route at a little café for a glass of wine or cup of coffee.

ZUG

About midway between Zürich and Lucerne, facing Lake Zug, is one of Switzerland's oldest sites, the charming town of Zug. The medieval section that remains hugs the water's edge where the boats come in to dock. From the lake the streets weave back through the colorful old medieval gabled houses with overhanging balconies. However, excavations have shown that Zug's history goes back far beyond the Middle Ages—it dates as far back as the Neolithic era.

ZÜRICH

In Zürich there is much to see and do. On a warm day we suggest taking an excursion on one of the steamers that ply lovely Lake Zürich. There is a schedule posted at each of the piers stating where the boats go and when they depart. During the summer there is frequent service and a wide selection to suit your mood and your time frame.

Zürich is also a great city for just meandering through the medieval section with its maze of tiny twisting streets, colorful squares, charming little shops, and tempting cafés. It is fun to walk down the promenade by the River Limmat to the lake front and cross over the Quaibrücke (bridge) to return by the opposite bank. When weary, cross back over one of the bridges that span the river to complete your circle.

For those of you who like museums, the Swiss National Museum has a display depicting Swiss civilization from prehistoric times to the modern day. Zürich's Fine Arts Museum is well worth a visit. Of special interest here are some of the paintings of Ferdinand Hodler, one of the finest Swiss artists of the early 20th century. Also on display are some of the paintings of a favorite Swiss artist, Anker, whose delightful paintings capture the warmth of family and home with simplicity and humor.

Cathedral buffs will enjoy the impressive Grossmünster whose construction dates back to the 11th century. This very imposing cathedral, built on a site originally occupied by a church built by Charlemagne, dominates Zürich with its two domed towers.

Medieval Switzerland

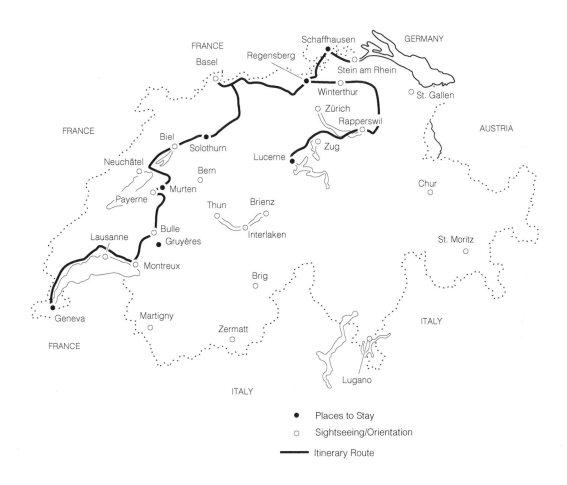

- ● Places to Stay
- ○ Sightseeing/Orientation
- ▬▬ Itinerary Route

Medieval Switzerland

Kapellbrücke, Lucerne

Switzerland has some of the most enchanting and remarkably well-preserved medieval villages and towns in Europe. Scattered across the countryside are towns whose character and atmosphere suggest a style of life that slipped by many centuries ago. Walled ramparts often enclose a maze of twisting, narrow streets, stone buildings, painted fountains, intricate clock towers, turrets, and a wealth of history. Sometimes capping the crest of a hill or perched precariously on a valley's ledge, these settlements captivate the imagination and are fascinating to explore.

This itinerary wanders from Lucerne to Geneva through glorious countryside and intriguing medieval towns. If you are the second-time-around traveler who has already followed the standard tourist trail between Zürich and Geneva via Lucerne and Interlaken and who would like to discover Switzerland with a different approach and emphasis, this itinerary might be perfect for you. Another possibility for this routing would be to use it in conjunction with the *Swiss Highlights* itinerary—the two dovetail perfectly to complete a circle of Switzerland. The true medieval village connoisseur among you will say that many of the walled villages have been left out. This is true—there are many others scattered throughout Switzerland, but these are some of my favorites and are spaced in such a way as to map a delightful journey.

ORIGINATING CITY   LUCERNE

Lucerne, with its magical setting, is a delightful starting point for this itinerary since it serves as a wonderful introduction to Switzerland and offers a tempting sampling of what is to come—lakes, mountains, a twisting river, wonderful bridges, colorful flowers, fountains, boats, decorative buildings, and a beautifully preserved old town.

Remnants of stone walls trace an outline around the old town of Lucerne. Although the ramparts that once encircled the city have deteriorated with time, the old section remains a marvelously preserved example of a medieval city—an exceptionally attractive one. Stately ancient buildings line the river, which winds through the town and meanders down to the lake, and architecturally lovely old bridges span its width. Built in the 14th century, the **Kapellbrücke** is one of the most famous of these bridges, and with its wooden roof, walls painted with murals, and even a little chapel midway, this delightful bridge has almost become the trademark of Lucerne.

DESTINATION I   REGENSBERG

From Lucerne head north towards Zürich. You might want to deviate from the highway about 20 minutes after leaving Lucerne to stop at the town of **Zug**, located at the north end of the **Zuger-See** (Lake Zug). Zug is a very old town with many buildings dating back to the 15th century. There is a small core of the old town that is a perfectly walled enclave entered through a gateway under the clock tower.

Soon after leaving Zug, change directions and follow a road heading south along Lake Zürich. Watch for signs to **Rapperswil**, located on a small peninsula jutting out into the lake. Rapperswil has a wonderful location on the banks of Lake Zürich, many colorful squares, and exceptionally preserved medieval buildings. A majestic castle on a rise in the middle of town contains the **Polish Museum**. During World War II many of the art treasures of Poland were smuggled out of the country and brought here for safekeeping. Many still remain and are on display at the museum.

From Rapperswil continue north for about 30 minutes to **Winterthur**. This is quite a large commercial city, but the central section still retains a great deal of medieval charm. The most interesting area is near the train station. Nearby, one of the main streets has been closed to all but pedestrian traffic and has a variety of shops housed in quaint medieval buildings. Only a short walk farther on is one of the most famous museums in Switzerland, the **Galerie Oskar Reinhart**, a truly exquisite small museum. It houses works by famous European artists from the 18th to the 20th centuries beautifully displayed in lovely natural lighting. Especially enjoyable are the paintings by Anker who captured the warmth and charm of family life in Switzerland. The museum is usually closed on Monday mornings and every day from noon to 2 pm.

From Winterthur head west toward Bulach—about a 20-minute drive. Upon arrival in Bulach carefully follow the signs heading west towards Dielsdorf—another 10 minutes beyond Bulach. The town of Regensberg is just on the western outskirts of Dielsdorf, perched on a nearby hilltop.

Regensberg is very special. Within only a few kilometers of Zürich, this perfectly preserved medieval village sits crowning a small hill. Vineyards climb up to the little community whose atmosphere beckons you back 500 years. Lodged in this romantic village is one of the most exquisite little inns in Switzerland, the **Rote Rose**.

An excursion to circle some of the walled villages in the Regensberg area might also prove of interest. It is only about a 20-minute drive to the ancient spa town of **Baden**. As you approach Baden it looks like a rather industrial town, but venture farther and head for the core of the old village where you will discover, hovering above the banks of the River Limmat, the charm of yesteryear. Baden has many wonderful old gaily painted houses with steep roofs and dormer windows, which step down the hillside in columns until the last row becomes the riverbank itself. A covered wooden bridge forms a picturesque scene at the middle of the old section of town, and a church with a high steeple sets the backdrop to the picture. This spa town of Baden has been famous since

Regensberg

Medieval Switzerland 63

Roman times and its waters are especially popular for the treatment of arthritis.

From Baden drive on to **Aarau**, another beautifully preserved medieval town. Like Baden, as you approach the town, it looks like an industrial city, as indeed it is, being famous for textiles. However, the center of the old town is delightful, with narrow, twisting streets, colorful houses with steep brown roofs, frequently with fresco decorations under the eaves, and carved little bay windows jutting out over the tiny streets. Aarau is a perfect town for strolling.

DESTINATION II   SCHAFFHAUSEN

Assuming Regensberg as your point of departure, it is a short drive on to **Schaffhausen**. Even with a leisurely departure you can plan on an arrival in time for lunch at the wonderful **Rheinhotel Fischerzunft**, aptly named because it has a superb location right on the pedestrian promenade running along the Rhine. There is interesting sightseeing in the Schaffhausen area and the Rheinhotel Fischerzunft is a delightful place to stay. If you really want a special stay, request a suite overlooking the river.

The town of Schaffhausen is a well preserved, walled, medieval city which developed as a result of the Rhine traffic and the commerce it brought. To the west of town is the **Rheinfall** (waterfall) whose cascading waters halted the flow of river traffic. Arrangements had to be made to circumvent the falls and transport the cargo by land, so, as a result, Schaffhausen grew to accommodate the tradesmen with housing and food. In town are a number of painted houses with quaint projecting windows called oriel windows. There are also several delightful fountains, old towers, and a castle on a knoll above the city. While in Schaffhausen you will certainly want to make the very short excursion to see the Rheinfall. Where the water comes crashing down, there is a park and a concession where you can take a boat right out to the base of the falls.

Another excursion from Schaffhausen is a visit to the walled town of **Stein am Rhein**. Although packed with tourists during the summer season, it nevertheless looks like a fairytale village, with each building almost completely covered in colorful paintings and designs. An option would be to take the ferry from Schaffhausen to Stein am Rhein for lunch and make it a day's outing. Ferry schedules are available at the Rheinhotel Fischerzunft and at the ticket booth on the dock, just steps from your hotel.

Stein am Rhein

DESTINATION III   SOLOTHURN

To reach Solothurn from Schaffhausen, head south following the signs for Zürich, but before entering the city, turn west, following the signs to Basel, a convenient stop on the way to Solothurn. **Basel**, in spite of its size, still retains a wonderful ambiance of days long gone. As you approach, the old section of town is easy to find, identified by the two towering spires of the cathedral. From the Münsterplatz you can explore most of the old section on foot.

From Basel it is a short and easy drive to Solothurn. **Solothurn** might appear unattractive on the outskirts, but once you pass through the medieval wall, the modern world is left behind and you enter a sector of the town that transports you back through the centuries. You should not have a problem finding the **Hotel Krone**—it is on one of the main streets and faces the plaza in front of the large **Saint Ursen Cathedral**. The bedrooms in the main building are spacious and nicely decorated. In the newer wing which stretches behind the hotel the rooms are much smaller, but these are mostly for singles' use. The main dining room at the Krone is charming and always busy with not only tourists, but also the local citizens. The Krone seems to be the center for much of the social life in town with wedding receptions, business meetings, and parties.

Solothurn is one of the oldest Roman settlements in the Alps and with its many squares, fountains, and colorful buildings, it is a fun town for meandering. It will not take you long to see the whole town so I would suggest some other sightseeing excursions from Solothurn. One day, drive up into the **Jura Mountains** to visit the little walled town of **Saint Ursanne**, which you enter by crossing the river and passing through quaint gates. Saint Ursanne is located in a beautiful section of Switzerland famous for horse breeding and in summer splendid-looking horses graze in the rolling green meadows and adorable colts frolic in the fields.

Another excursion from Solothurn is a visit to **Bern**, a wonderful old city brimming with whimsical fountains, colorful squares, arcaded shops, and perfectly preserved medieval buildings.

DESTINATION IV   MURTEN

Although it is just a short drive from Solothurn to Murten, there are a couple of walled villages along the way. Leaving Solothurn, take the highway west toward Biel, another picturesque medieval town, but if time is short, it might be best to bypass it and continue directly on to the tiny town of **La Neuveville**, a pretty walled village on the banks of Lake Biel. Near La Neuveville is **Saint Peter's Island** where Jean-Jacques Rousseau stayed in 1765. By taking a boat from La Neuveville, it is possible to visit the island and see the house where Rousseau lived. Farther along the shore from La Neuveville is another outstanding miniature walled village, **Le Landeron**. In summer both Le Landeron and La Neuveville are sensational, with masses of flowers, picturesque buildings, brightly painted fountains, clock towers, little antique shops, and outdoor cafés. But do not linger too long—your next destination is even more inviting. **Murten**, snuggled along the banks of **Lake Murten**, is a fairy-tale village and the best vantage point for viewing it is from the top of the surrounding ramparts. The town deserves to be explored lazily to fully enjoy the twisting little streets, fountains, old buildings, and little squares.

If you want to surround yourself with the ambiance of days gone by, stay at the **Hotel Weisses Kreuz,** a superbly run small, family-owned hotel with rooms tucked into a cluster of characterful old buildings in the heart of the old town. Within walking distance from the encircling medieval walls, on the water's edge is the pleasing **Hotel Schiff**.

Murten

Also snuggled on the lake, in Meyriez, but within driving distance of town, is the deluxe, exquisitely appointed **Le Vieux Manoir au Lac.** All hotels are excellent—the choice would depend upon your preference as to location, level of luxury, and price.

DESTINATION V GRUYÈRES

Your next destination, the picturesque town of Gruyères, is just a short drive along the main highway from Murten. To extend your journey and include some sightseeing into your day, I would suggest the following detours. First, instead of returning to the main highway, drive south along Lake Murten. Soon after you pass the south end of the lake, you come to **Avenches**. It is hard to believe as you look at this sleepy little hamlet of about 2,000 that in the 1st and 2nd centuries it was a powerful Roman city boasting a population of over 20,000. You can grasp the mood of this "lost city" of the Romans when you visit the amphitheater built to seat 10,000. In a tower over the amphitheater's entrance is a museum displaying some of the artifacts found in the excavations and an interesting pottery collection.

Another excursion en route to Gruyères would be to travel just south of Avenches to the town of **Payerne** and visit its famous 11th-century abbey. This Benedictine abbey is supposed to have been founded by the Empress Adelheid, wife of Emperor Otto I. The church is one of the finest examples of Romanesque architecture in Switzerland, with simple lines but marvelous proportions and use of golden limestone and gray sandstone.

Romont, a small walled medieval town, is also on the way to Gruyères. To reach Romont it is necessary to travel the small country roads leading southeast from Payerne—about a half hour's drive. The town was built by Peter II of Savoy in the 13th century and occupies a very picturesque site on the knoll overlooking the Glane Valley. From Romont continue southeast on the small road toward Bulle. Just beyond Bulle the small town of **Gruyères** will appear ahead of you crowning the top of a miniature mountain.

Gruyères

To reach Gruyères you wind up the little road toward the village, but you cannot take your car into the town as it is closed to traffic (there are several car parks on the approach to town). The **Hostellerie des Chevaliers** is located just above the car park at the entrance to town. Guestrooms at the rear of the hotel look up to the medieval walls and have lovely views of lush green meadows backed by beautiful mountains. On the cobbled square of Gruyères we recommend a delightful hotel, the **Hostellerie de Saint Georges**.

Gruyères is such a postcard-perfect village that it attracts busloads of visitors who crowd the small main street during the day. However, most of the tourists leave at night and the town regains its fairy-tale quality. Plan excursions during the day to avoid the bustle of the midday tourist rush and return in the evening to this idyllic Swiss village which is then yours to enjoy. One possible outing would be to go to the small **cheese museum** just at the bottom of the hill from Gruyères. In the museum (which is also a cheese factory) demonstrations are given on how cheeses are made in the various Swiss cantons. There is also a movie (in English) with an explanation of the process. Cheese enthusiasts might want to linger in this area and take more short excursions to visit other little villages and sample their dairy products—you might come home a little plumper, but a connoisseur of delicious Swiss cheese.

Other side trips that might be appealing would be to travel the distance to **Lake Geneva** and explore the many quaint little towns along the lake. Of course, the ever-pleasurable lake rides can be picked up from most of the lakeside towns. From Gruyères you can easily visit the famous **Castle of Chillon** located on a tiny peninsula jutting into Lake Geneva just beyond Montreux. This castle originally belonged to the Counts of Savoy, but its great fame came from Lord Byron's famous poem *The Prisoner of Chillon*.

When it is time to leave Gruyères, there are several options. It is just a short drive around Lake Geneva to Geneva where there are train connections to all over Europe plus international flights. Or it is an easy trip to complete your "medieval" circle and return to Lucerne via the beautiful **Simmental Valley**, stopping along the way to visit the walled town of **Thun** where you can take one of the lake steamers to Interlaken.

Mountain Adventures

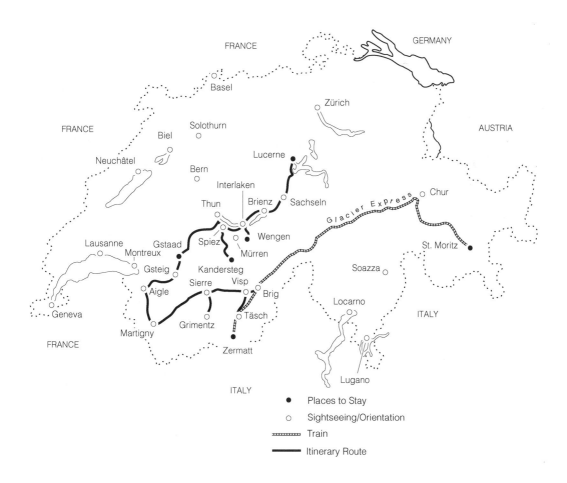

Mountain Adventures

Kandersteg

This itinerary is for the true mountain lover, for the traveler whose year will be happier for the memory of a perfect sunset over a snow-capped mountain peak, whose problems will shrink into perspective as the mind wanders back to gentle meadows splashed with wildflowers, whose tensions will fade as the soul recalls the stroll up a quiet mountain path. To enjoy this itinerary, you need not be an Olympic champion, just take pleasure in being outdoors. You will be in style as long as you have one common denominator—love of the mountains. Of course, if you are a mountain climber, the beckoning of the Matterhorn will probably be overwhelming and I wish for you a perfect few days to obtain your goal. If you enjoy skiing, then the slopes of Gstaad will be irresistible. However, if you simply like to meander down quiet trails dappled with sunlight, and your idea of exertion is to stoop to pick a flower, this itinerary is also perfect for you. The mountain resorts of Switzerland teem with European hikers enjoying the mountain air and walking trails. These holiday seekers for the most part are not your image of the disciplined, trim, serious athlete. Most hikers are couples or families dressed in woolen sweaters, corduroy knickers, bright knee socks, and sturdy walking shoes, and equipped with walking sticks, laughing and talking as they meander along the trails. Therefore, feel most comfortable, no matter what your ability, to join this jovial, friendly group of "mountaineers."

If time is limited, you can follow the routing from Lucerne to Zermatt and end your trip there. Return to Lucerne or Zürich or Geneva, or else head south to the Swiss-Italian Lake District. However, if you can possibly extend your holiday, try the Glacier Express, a privately owned train connecting Zermatt and Saint Moritz. This all-day train ride over some of the most glorious mountain passes in the world is a highlight of any trip to Switzerland. Even if the visibility is zero, the journey on this little red train will still be fun. What a memorable experience to arrive at the train station in Zermatt by horse and sleigh (or horse and buggy in summer), climb onto the train, settle down in the clean, bright compartment, enjoy a gourmet meal in the Victorian dining car, chat and laugh with fellow passengers, and arrive relaxed and happy in Saint Moritz.

Include all of these mountain villages or, if time is short, select the resorts that sound most suited to you. Switzerland is blessed with Alpine heights, and to visit Switzerland is to enjoy her mountains. Don't go home without strolling along some of the paths and soaking up fabulous mountain vistas.

ORIGINATING CITY   LUCERNE

Because there are no international airports in the high mountain areas, this itinerary begins in one of Switzerland's most famous cities, **Lucerne**, a charming medieval town with a fairy-tale setting—directly on the lake with a beautiful mountain backdrop. Although Lucerne does not have its own airport, there is a direct train from the Zürich airport, a quick and convenient journey taking just over an hour. Spend a few days in

Lucerne relaxing before heading south into the mountains. We highly recommend the **Romantik Hotel Wilden Mann**, located in the romantic old part of Lucerne, as a superb introduction to the wonders of Switzerland. Another choice for Lucerne is the **Hotel des Balances** located directly on the River Reuss. Both hotels are convenient for exploring Lucerne on foot, so no matter which hotel you choose, wait until you are ready to begin your driving itinerary before picking up your car.

DESTINATION I   WENGEN

Today's destination is the town of Wengen in the region of the famous **Jungfrau**. The drive is easy and very beautiful. An early departure would be best, enabling you to linger along the way. Head south from Lucerne toward Hergswil. Near Stansstad follow the highway south toward Brienz—on your way you will pass through the town of **Sachseln**, located on Lake Sarner about midway between Lucerne and Brienz. This is a good stopping point if you want to include a coffee break with a little sightseeing. Sachseln is very famous, for in the center of town is a beautiful church where **Saint Nicholas of Flüe** is buried. From Sachseln follow the highway to Brienz and then on to Interlaken. At Interlaken follow the signs south toward Lauterbrunnen, where you will be leaving your car and board a train for the last leg of your journey.

If it is still early in the day, before parking in Lauterbrunnen drive south for a few more kilometers, watching for a sign on the left side of the road for the **Trümmelbachfälle**, one of the most unusual waterfalls in the world. Park you car at the designated area near the road. From there it is just a very short walk over to the entrance to the falls—yes, "entrance." In the side of the mountain a steel door opens to an elevator that ascends within the mountain. When you get out, follow the path that winds down the hillside, snaking in and out of the mountain en route. Along the way you see ten dramatic waterfalls, gigantic, powerful thrusts of water gushing down from the Eiger, Mönch, and Jungfrau glaciers through twisted fissures in the rock. As you walk along the roaring water, there are balconies at various levels, strategically placed for photos and viewing.

In the darker recesses, the falls are illuminated, increasing even further the magic of the experience. The whole outing should not take more than about an hour. However, if you are in a hurry and there is a line waiting for the elevator, you can easily walk up the well-marked path for the same views.

Returning to **Lauterbrunnen** after your visit to the waterfall, park your car and board a train for the last leg of your journey. As usual, the Swiss are extremely efficient and have organized a number of visual aids to simplify the situation. The car park at Lauterbrunnen is well marked. Once your car is parked, follow the signs to the train station from which the trains leave frequently. The ride up from Lauterbrunnen to Wengen is just spectacular: as the train climbs from the valley you look down as from an airplane to the **Lauterbrunnen Valley**. The journey is truly magnificent, with cliff-like mountains rising steeply from the flat valley and mighty waterfalls cascading down the sides—very reminiscent of the Yosemite Valley in California. It is only a 15-minute ride up to Wengen but, on a clear day, 15 glorious minutes.

Wengen's location is spectacular—high on a mountain meadow overlooking the Lauterbrunnen Valley and beyond to the awe-inspiring mountains. This is a center for outdoor enthusiasts and sportsmen. From all over the world tourists come to soak up the mountain beauty. In winter skiing is the main attraction. In the milder months walking paths stretch out in every direction for the hiker, offering a new vista at every turn, each more beautiful than the last. Leisurely mountain viewing or gentle strolls are matched with the strenuous mountain climbs of the **Bernese Oberland** if you are adventuresome. Mountain guides can be hired to give you advice and assistance. Remember always to consult a local guide if you are planning any serious climbing.

We recommend two places to stay in Wengen: the **Alpenrose** and the **Regina**. We love them both. Study our descriptions in the hotel section and decide which one you prefer. If you call ahead and advise the hotel of your arrival time, they will send an electric cart to the train depot, or phone the hotel when you arrive and leave your luggage at the station to be retrieved later. You can walk to either hotel. The Regina is perched on the

Lauterbrunnen Valley and Staubbach Falls

hillside above and to the right of the train station and the Alpenrose is located on a small street down the hillside.

At either hotel, splurge and request one of the best rooms with a view balcony—the reward is an unforgettable mountain panorama. Both hotels are family-owned and family-operated and many guests return year after year to spend their holiday surrounded by fellow guests they have met in past years.

While staying in Wengen the prime sightseeing excursion is to visit the region of the **Jungfrau.** This is a circle trip taken by a series of little trains to the summit of the **Jungfraujoch.** Dominated by the Jungfrau, this boasts the highest train station in Europe and from its vantage point you will marvel at the spectacular vistas of the surrounding, awe-inspiring peaks. Known the world over, this trip is probably the most famous mountain sightseeing adventure in Switzerland—one you will not want to miss.

It will be difficult to leave the region of the Jungfrau, but when you can wrench yourself away more splendor awaits you. A short drive back to Interlaken brings you again to the main highway circling the south side of Lake Thun. When you arrive at Interlaken, travel west in the direction of Spiez. Just off the main road that travels between Interlaken and Thun, **Spiez** is worth a short detour before leaving the lake and heading south through a lovely Alpine valley in the direction of Kandersteg. With the Alpine peaks and the lake as a magnificent backdrop, the village of Spiez lies on the shore of its own picturesque bay with a little marina and is crowned by a medieval castle.

From Spiez travel south on a road that winds along the path of the River Kander, through the beautiful Kandersteg Valley. The road and its journey end at Kandersteg.

Spiez

In **Kandersteg** we recommend two hotels that are both owned and managed by the Maeder family. Both of their hotels are tucked at the very end of the valley after the road has traveled through the center of town. With their two properties the Maeders offer the traveler a choice in accommodation in terms of ambiance and price. The **Waldhotel Doldenhorn** is a lovely hotel with 34 rooms and a fine restaurant. By contrast, the **Landgasthof Ruedihus** is a smaller, more intimate inn. Whereas the Doldenhorn is larger and a bit more sophisticated, the Landgasthof Ruedihus—very old, with only a few rooms, a lovely restaurant, and a cozy *stubli*—is so charming that it will win your heart immediately.

Kandersteg makes an excellent base both for sightseeing and enjoying the natural wonders of the area. Hiking is especially appealing. Numerous walks lead off every point of the compass, each more tempting than the last. At the end of the village a chairlift rises from the valley to **Lake Oeschinen** where rugged cliffs jut dramatically at the edge of the clear mountain lake. The lake lies below the terminal of the chairlift and is reached via a beautiful path through mountain meadows. On a clear day a lovely outing is to walk down the mountain rather than take the chairlift on the return to Kandersteg. Another excursion from Kandersteg is to drive to the end of the other fork of the valley to the town of Adelboden. To do this, it is necessary to retrace the road a short distance to the town of Frutigen. At this town take the Engstligental Valley road branching off to the left. This is a beautiful drive terminating at **Adelboden**, an attractive resort village with many old wooden farmhouses nestled on the hillside. Again, there is a fantastic backdrop of majestic mountain peaks. As you return to Kandersteg, on the right-hand side of the road are signs to the **Blausee** (Blue Lake). Park your car near the main road and walk along a wooded path through a forest of twisted, mysterious trees. You begin to wonder where in the world you are going when suddenly you come upon a tiny, gorgeous lake—a photographer's dream. The incredibly blue, clear lake is set in the forest with a jagged Alpine horizon. There are usually many people here, as it is a favorite excursion of the Swiss who like to come to eat lunch on the side of the lake in a little chalet-type restaurant, with tables set out on the terrace on mild days. This is also a popular stop for families with children who enjoy taking one of the boat rides or just circling the lake on the twisting little path following the shoreline amongst the gnarled forest. The effect is rather like a scene from *Hansel and Gretel*.

Kandersteg is also well known as the point at which the road ends and only the train continues on to the Rhône Valley. For those traveling by car in this direction the car can be put "piggy-back" on the train for the ride through the mountains to Brig.

DESTINATION III   GSTAAD

It is not a long journey from Kandersteg to Gstaad. Retrace the half-hour drive back toward Spiez, and almost as soon as you reach the main road running along the shore of Lake Thun, there is a branch off to the west that follows the lovely Simmental Valley. In less than an hour you should reach the turnoff to Gstaad and then it is only another few minutes' drive into town. There are many places to stay in **Gstaad**, but our favorites are the charming **Post Hotel Rössli**, a former postal station of weathered wood, **Le Grand Chalet**, a delightful chalet-style hotel, and the **Hotel Olden**, a gaily-painted inn. The Post Hotel Rössli and Hotel Olden are on the main street in the pedestrian center of town. Le Grand Chalet is just a short walk away, on a hillside above the village. Ruedi Widmer, the proprietor of the Post Hotel Rössli, is a celebrated local mountaineer and has a reputation as an excellent ski guide. Only about 7 kilometers from Gstaad, in the town of Schönried, is another winner: the beautiful **Hotel Alpenrose** with beautifully decorated guestrooms and splendid mountain views.

In spite of the fact that it has an international reputation as a very chic ski resort catering to the wealthy jet set, Gstaad retains much of its old-world, small-town, charming simplicity. The setting of Gstaad is magnificent with the surrounding rugged mountain peaks. In summer the hiking or mountain climbing is excellent and in winter Gstaad offers one of the most famous networks of trails for skiing.

From Gstaad, continue on the road south through the small picturesque village of Gsteig. Gsteig is situated at the end of the valley, and from this point the road climbs sharply past Les Diablerets and on to the town of Le Sépey. At Le Sépey travel southwest toward

Zermatt

Aigle, where you then travel south along the Rhône Valley in the direction of Martigny.

At Martigny follow the river as it winds northeast toward Sierre. If you are in the mood for adventure, when you reach Sierre, watch for the turnoff to the Val d'Anniviers and follow the road south, following signs to Grimentz. The narrow road twists and turns up the mountain. When you come to Vissoie, turn right to **Grimentz**, a fantastic Valais village clinging to a mountain ridge. It is an especially pretty sight in summer, with exuberant displays of brilliant-red geraniums that seem even more vibrant in contrast to the age-blackened wood of the antique chalets. Stop here to enjoy a fondue at the **Hotel de Moiry** before retracing your way back to the Rhône Valley where you continue east toward Brig. At Brig you can turn in your rental car (arrange this in advance) and pick up the Glacier Express to Saint Moritz.

DEVIATION: If you are not planning to take the Glacier Express and want to keep your car, instead of continuing to Brig, turn right (south) off the highway at Visp and follow signs to Zermatt. Cars are not allowed in Zermatt, so you have to park by the railway station in Täsch and board the train for the your journey to Zermatt.

For those of you who plan to continue the rest of your journey by train, turn in your rental car at Brig and then board the train for Zermatt. There are frequent trains that usually leave at 23 minutes after each hour for the ride, which takes about an hour and 20 minutes. Sit down and relax—the ride through the valley is glorious, ending only when the valley comes to a halt, blocked by the mighty peaks enclosing Zermatt.

Advance hotel reservations are a must in **Zermatt**. Although there are many hotels, there are also many tourists competing for the prime space. We have many recommendations listed for you in the hotel section. Each has its own personality and each is quite wonderful in its own way.

DESTINATION V   SAINT MORITZ

Be sure to spend several days in Zermatt. If you enjoy walking, there are endless possibilities. Not only do trails spider-web out of the village in every direction, but trams and cable cars climb the mountains, tempting you to wander through the glorious high mountain meadows.

When it is time to leave Zermatt, a real treat lies in store—the **Glacier Express**, a privately owned train that departs Zermatt in the morning heading north to Brig, then continues east, threading through the end of the Rhône Valley, passing through the Furka Pass Tunnel, climbing over the Oberalppass and the Albulapass, before dropping down into Saint Moritz. This jolly, bright-red train is the perfect way to traverse this spectacular, awe-inspiring route. Seats, however, must be reserved in advance. If you want to enjoy the fun of eating lunch in the quaint, wood-paneled, Victorian dining car, this also must be prearranged. You can do it at the same time you book your seat or by calling the Swiss Dining Car Company in Chur, Switzerland, tel: (081) 252 14 25. Reservations for the Glacier Express can be made through Rail Europe (visit our website, *www.karenbrown.com*, and click on Rail Europe) or, in the United States, through your travel agent. Outside of the USA, check with Switzerland Tourism for where to make reservations.

10:10 am depart Zermatt via the Glacier Express
6:11 pm arrive Saint Moritz

Saint Moritz is one of the most popular of the jet-set ski areas, attracting the rich and famous from around the world. The town has an outstanding setting—one side backs onto the ski slopes, the other looks down to a lovely lake. Due to the popularity of the area, many hotels have sprung up to accommodate the tourists who flock here summer and winter. Saint Moritz is fun. It is a great place to shop in the designer boutiques and to people watch, especially in winter when many celebrities come to stay at the luxurious Palace Hotel. If money doesn't matter, you too might want to splurge at the Palace Hotel, but we suggest three smaller places to stay. Right in the center of town there are two family-run hotels—both excellent choices: the **Hotel Eden** and the **Hotel Languard**. If you prefer a more country ambiance, the **Meierei Landhotel**, a bishop's farm dating back to the 1600s, might interest you. It is situated in a meadow, across the lake looking back at Saint Moritz.

When you are ready to complete your holiday, you can take a train back to Zürich or perhaps continue by bus (the Palm Express, see page 21 for contact information) to Lugano.

Mountain Adventures

Best on a Budget

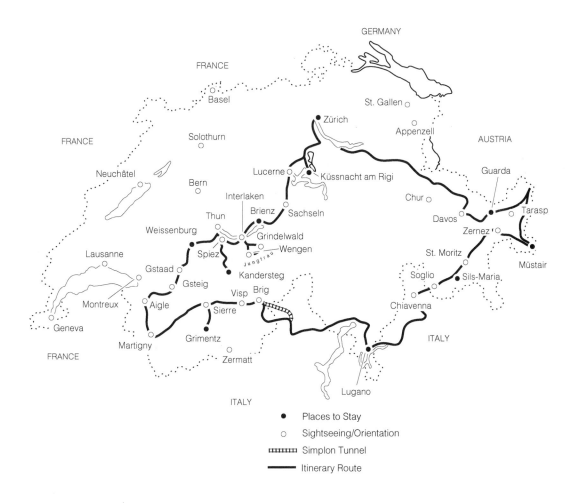

GERMANY

FRANCE

Basel

St. Gallen

FRANCE

Zürich

Appenzell

AUSTRIA

Solothurn

Neuchâtel

Lucerne

Küssnacht am Rigi

Guarda

Bern

Chur

Tarasp

Interlaken

Brienz

Sachseln

Davos

Zernez

Thun

Grindelwald

Müstair

Weissenburg

Spiez

Wengen

St. Moritz

Lausanne

Gstaad

Jungfrau

Soglio

Sils-Maria

Montreux

Gsteig

Kandersteg

Chiavenna

Aigle

Visp

Brig

Geneva

Sierre

ITALY

FRANCE

Martigny

Grimentz

Zermatt

ITALY

Lugano

- ● Places to Stay
- ○ Sightseeing/Orientation
- ⊞⊞⊞⊞ Simplon Tunnel
- —— Itinerary Route

Best on a Budget

Soglio

This itinerary was a last-minute inspiration. Just as *Switzerland: Charming Inns & Itineraries* went to press in its first edition, Barbara Tapp, our illustrator, was studying photographs we had taken of Swiss hotels with the purpose of finding material to assist her with the hotel sketches. Coming across a photo of Hotel du Lac Seehof that we had put in the reject file, Barbara asked why we weren't including this "beautiful little lakefront inn." We gently explained to her that the hotel was not quite of the caliber of the others in the guide—it was just too "modest." The building was attractive but not an architectural masterpiece, the rooms were very clean but quite small. Barbara then asked the price—it was extremely low. "Oh, you must include it," she said. "This is just the type of hotel my husband Richard and I would adore. Our budget would stretch so much further. We could stay a week with meals for what a few days would cost in some of the deluxe hotels for room only." Barbara asked if we had others in the inexpensive category that were not going to be included. Actually, we had been intrigued by several small inns found off the beaten path, such as the Hotel de Moiry in the medieval village of Grimentz. Barbara's enthusiasm for the qualities of these "little gems" was contagious. So this itinerary is for my friend Barbara and for others, young at heart, adventurous in spirit, and traveling on a budget. Prices have gone up since our first edition, but the value received in these small inns is still outstanding.

ORIGINATING CITY   ZÜRICH

Zürich makes a convenient starting point for any holiday in Switzerland. Trains from all over Europe pull into Zürich's central station and airplanes from around the world land at its conveniently located airport. If you arrive by plane, it is so easy and economical to just take the train directly from the airport to the center of Zürich. We have a selection of hotels here, but none of them is inexpensive, so if you are on a tight budget, you might want to leave the city without stopping overnight.

DESTINATION I   KÜSSNACHT AM RIGI

From Zürich, head south out of town in the direction of Lucerne. About 35 kilometers after leaving the city, the road merges into the N4, which you follow all the way to **Küssnacht am Rigi**, a small village located on a northern finger of **Lake Lucerne**. The **Hotel du Lac Seehof**, owned and managed by the fifth generation of the Trutmann family, has a stellar position right on the lake, adjacent to the ferry landing. The bedrooms are pleasant—some of the more deluxe have antique decor—and good value for money. The hotel has an inside dining room, but it is the lakeside terrace that is most entrancing—on balmy evenings it is superb to linger over a romantic dinner under the trees with the lights gently reflecting in the water.

You can climb aboard one of the many ferries that ply Lake Lucerne from the pier in front of the Hotel du Lac Seehof. There are many charming towns you can visit by boat but the prize, which should not be missed, is **Lucerne**. Plan to spend one day there as a side trip from Küssnacht, exploring the maze of little lanes in the old town, and cross back and forth over the colorful bridges that span the River Reuss, which winds through the center of the town.

Another budget recommendation is the charming **Swiss Chalet** in the nearby town of Merlischachen.

DESTINATION II   BRIENZ

From Küssnacht am Rigi travel south of Lucerne to a spectacularly beautiful region of lakes and mountains. Two lakes, **Lake Brienz** and **Lake Thun**, hinged by a speck of land referred to as Interlaken, are surrounded by towering peaks that reach to the heights of the ever-famous Jungfrau. Nestled on the shores of the lake that bears its name is the charming town of **Brienz** whose web of old narrow streets shadowed by dark wooden chalet-style houses and shops is fun to explore. This is a great wood-carving center and most of the carvings available for purchase throughout Switzerland come from this dear lakeside town. Brienz is also famous for its violin-making school. On the hillside, in a residential district just above town, is a charming, reasonably priced inn, the **Chalet Hotels Schönegg & Spycher Garni**. The guestrooms in the weathered old Chalet Schönegg are especially appealing in their Alpine decor and charm. It is an easy walk into town from the hotel but it is tempting to relax and settle in as the views from this hillside location, overlooking the town and across the lake, are spectacular.

Chalet Schönegg, Brienz

With Brienz as a base you have a wealth of excursions to choose from. For a breathtaking, panoramic view of the Bernese Alps and Lake Brienz, consider a journey on the **Brienz Rothorn Bahn**. This wonderful old steam locomotive traverses beautiful scenery on its ascent by rack railway to the summit (2,350 meters) of the Rothorn. The round-trip journey requires approximately three hours and departs from the lakeside town of Brienz. There is also a hotel at the summit, functional in its decor and comfort, where one can dine or spend the night: Hotel Rothorn Kulm, tel: (033) 951 12 21.

In the vicinity of Brienz there are several falls that cascade down near the heavily wooded water's edge, the most famous of which, the **Giessbach Falls**, are accessible by train from the Brienz station and a funicular. If you venture out to Giessbach, allow time for lunch or tea on the terrace of the lovely **Grandhotel Giessbach** located right next to the falls and enjoy gorgeous views of the lake.

On the outskirts of Brienz, located by the **Wyssensee**, **Ballenberg** is a marvelous museum that should be incorporated into anyone's travels in Switzerland. Set on a vast acreage of lush meadow and fields planted with grain and flowers, this open-air museum offers a wonderful introduction to the regional architecture and cultures of Switzerland. Historical buildings representative of the different cantons have been relocated to this site and you can wander the park on a path that journeys from canton to canton. People work the museum dressed in costume and set the scene of an era centuries ago.

DESTINATION III   KANDERSTEG

The drive around the lake from Brienz and back into the mountain valley to the village of Kandersteg is beautiful. Perhaps the most spectacular portion is when you pass through the scenic area surrounding the famous resort of Interlaken, strategically located on a bridge of land connecting two of Switzerland's most beautiful small lakes, Lake Thun and Lake Brienz. Follow the road that traces the southern rim of the lakes. Before reaching the town of Spiez, watch for a turnoff for a road heading south into the Kandersteg Valley. Beyond the town of Reichenbach, watch for a sign on the right side of the road for the **Blausee** (Blue Lake). Park your car and, on foot, follow the wooded, scenic pathway to this gem of a little lake with its curtain of rocks rising in the background. One wonders how nature can compose such magic. For those who are ready for a snack, there is a charming little chalet-style restaurant nestled along the shore. The Blausee is very popular and will be crowded if the day is nice—especially with families, since this tiny lake appeals to the little ones.

From the Blausee, continue to **Kandersteg**. The road actually ends in this typical Swiss village—to continue farther you would have to take a train through the mountains. Kandersteg enjoys a splendid setting of meadows and towering Alpine peaks. People come to this gorgeous spot to hike and there is a wealth of trails for all levels of ability.

On arrival in Kandersteg, continue right through the heart of this small town to its outskirts. When you have traveled about as far as the road will take you, off to its right-hand side you will see a picture-perfect small chalet, the **Landgasthof Ruedihus**, which not only abounds with charm, but also is an excellent value. This flower-bedecked gem is one of the oldest chalets in the valley and has been restored to perfection, not only outside, but inside too, with antiques and pretty country fabrics being used in the decor. This charming inn has two restaurants, one upstairs, more formal in decor and gourmet in menu, the other off the entry, cozy under wooden beams. This second restaurant, the *stubli*, is a gathering spot for locals as well as resident guests and has a menu with a wonderful offering of raclette and fondue. This would prove a memorable spot to sample either of these, Switzerland's most popular dishes.

Now world-famous, fondue needs little introduction—melted Gruyères cheese, white wine, garlic, and kirsch are brought to the table in a chafing dish and diners use long forks to dip squares of bread into the delectable mixture. Raclette is a countryman's dinner. A block of Bagnes cheese is softened over a fire then the top of the block is scraped onto your plate and traditionally served with boiled potatoes and onions. Sometimes variations in the accompaniment are offered, such as mushrooms, tomatoes, ham, or sausage.

There are many side trips that beckon from Kandersteg—you will certainly want to include the **Jungfraujoch Excursion**. This train ride to the base of the Jungfrau (see map and details in the Sightseeing Reference section) is one of Switzerland's highlights.

There are other wonderful possibilities for sightseeing in the area. With Kandersteg as your base, it is a short drive into **Interlaken** where you can meander through the town enjoying the ambiance of this Victorian-style resort. Better yet, take a lake excursion either on **Lake Thun** or **Lake Brienz**. Also highly recommended is a jaunt to see the medieval town of **Thun** with its dramatic castle perched on the hillside. A covered wooden staircase leading up to it adds to the fun of visiting the castle. For gift shoppers, Thun has an interesting shopping street with a mall of shops on an upper level and an elevated sidewalk.

DESTINATION IV   WEISSENBURG

After your stay in the mountain village of Kandersteg, retrace your way to the main highway and continue west following the Simmental Valley toward Gstaad. The **Hotel Alte Post**, an old coaching inn, is a charming country hotel in **Weissenburg**, on the road between the international resort of Gstaad and the magnificent mountain and lake district of Interlaken. The hotel backs onto the rushing torrents of the River Simme. You enter the hotel from the street into a small informal entry off which to one side is a simple country restaurant decorated with pine tables and benches and lovely painted beams. On the other side is a more formal restaurant, elegant in decor and table settings. At the back of the inn is a very informal dining area whose tables are set against windows with views of the rushing waters of the Simme. Guestrooms are very rustic in their decor, with wood-paneled walls and ceilings and country antiques—very reminiscent of a country *ferme auberge*. The sound of the road traffic is diminished by the time it reaches the top floor and any sound that could possibly be heard from guestrooms at the back is drowned out by the rushing river.

Weathered Old Barn Hung with Cow Bells near Gsteig

With Weissenburg as a base, be certain to visit the charming resort of **Gstaad**, then in about 15 minutes you will come to **Gsteig**, which shares the same glorious valley as Gstaad but not the same "jet-set" prices. The town of Gsteig is quaint, although without fancy restaurants. This is also a lush farming region and I'll always remember the weathered old chalets whose eaves are hung heavy with treasured cow bells.

One day enjoy an excursion to **Gruyères**, a charming little picture-book medieval village hugging the top of a small hill—really only one main street full of picturesque buildings. Surrounding this "toy town" are incredibly green meadows that seem to flow up to the mountains—it is a scene from *Heidi*. The town is famous for its wonderful cheeses and creams as Gruyères is in one of the excellent dairy regions of Switzerland. If you go to Gruyères, be sure to stop at a local restaurant for some quiche and, when in season, some berries smothered in unbelievably thick cream.

DESTINATION V   GRIMENTZ

After leaving Weissenburg, your next stop is the tiny town of Grimentz. The drive from Gsteig to Grimentz is beautiful, but involves mountainous driving and the route is recommended only after the snows have melted. As you leave Gsteig, follow the road that begins almost immediately to climb up into the mountains. The road twists over the mountains, passes through the town of Les Diablerets and the ski resort of Villars, and then winds down into the Rhône Valley. Upon reaching the main highway turn east and when you reach Sierre, follow the signs for the road heading south to Grimentz.

The town of **Grimentz** nestles on a side of the mountain overlooking the valley and beyond to the high Alpine peaks. The village is a masterpiece of perfection, with almost all of the buildings constructed in the traditional Valais style with dark weathered wood, slate roofs, and balconies. All this is set off in summer by masses of brilliant red geraniums. The **Hotel de Moiry**, found on the edge of town, is quite simple but, for the location, an excellent value. The Grimentz area is wonderful for high-mountain walking. From here it is possible to hike to neighboring villages and return by postal bus.

When it is time to leave Grimentz, get an early start because you have a long day's drive. Return to the main Highway 9, turn right (east), traveling through the Rhône Valley to Brig where you continue southeast on the 9, which takes you over the **Simplon Pass** into Italy. The first small town you come to across the border is Iselle, then about 22 kilometers farther you arrive in Domodossola. Although there is a short cut to the Swiss-Italian Lake District by following the turnoff near Domodossola through the Vigezzo Valley, I would suggest you stay on the main highway since the road is much better. Continue on toward Verbania and then follow the shoreline of Lake Maggiore through the picturesque town of **Ascona** (an excellent luncheon stop). Travel via Locarno to Bellinzona and then south via the freeway to Lugano. About a 20-minute drive south of Lugano, nestled on the west edge of Lake Lugano, you arrive at the picturesque village of Morcote.

To reach Morcote, go south from Lugano toward Milan on the road that traces the west edge of the lake. Morcote is the first exit you come to after the long tunnel. The heart of the village is so tiny that should have no difficulty finding the **Hotel Carina-Carlton**. However, once you arrive, you might have trouble finding a place to park. The town, which climbs steeply up the hill from the lake, shelters a maze of narrow alleyways — extremely quaint, but not easy to navigate by car. Best bet is to stop at the hotel (which is just across the road from the lake), leave your luggage, and then look for a place to park.

The Hotel Carina-Carlton makes a convenient hub for exploring this splendid romantic lake district. From the Morcote dock, just hop aboard one of the many ferries and spend your days discovering the charming villages snuggled along the lake. This part of Switzerland, where the houses are painted in soft pastel colors, makes you feel you are in Italy, and the gentle weather too is usually much kinder than you find farther north in the Swiss mountains. A boat excursion you must take is to Lugano, a wonderful medieval town. Another favorite outing is by ferry to Gandria, a tiny town that is so picturesque you won't be able to put your camera down.

If your holiday time has run out, then you could conveniently end your vacation in Morcote. You are just a short drive from the international airport at Milan or a pleasant train ride back to Zürich. However, if you can squeeze in a few more days, there is high adventure ahead. The southeastern region of Switzerland (the Grisons) offers some of the most spectacular scenery in the world.

From Morcote, return to Lugano and drive east into Italy. At the town of Menaggio turn north and drive along Lake Como. At the north end of the lake take the highway north toward the town of Chiavenna. The Swiss border appears just a few kilometers past Chiavenna and soon, high on a ledge to your left, you will spot the town of **Soglio** in the distance. This little town is one of the most dramatically beautiful in all of Switzerland— picture-perfect, typifying the classic image of a Swiss Alpine setting. A tiny community of just a few streets, its skyline dominated by a church spire, Soglio clings to a ledge high above the **Bregaglia Valley** and looks across to jagged peaks whose moods are affected dramatically by the time of the day. Early-morning light leaves a sliver of gold on the snowy escarpment enhanced by shifting clouds caressing the mountain peaks. The Alpine setting of Soglio is spectacular. There is not much to do in the village itself but, if you have time, linger here, relax, venture on a hike or two, and soak in the splendors and beauty of the setting which, we think, is one of the most outstanding in all of Switzerland.

From Soglio it is a beautiful drive following the path of the River Mera to the Silser See. On a peninsula of land that acts as a natural bridge between this lake and the Silvaplaner See is the hamlet of **Sils-Maria** and a lovely little pension, Pensiun Privata.

The **Pensiun Privata** is a charming inn and offers very reasonable accommodation. The pretty, four-storied, beige building with brown shutters is located on a small square in the village of Sils-Maria. Just to the left of the building is the gathering place for the colorful horse-drawn carriages that take guests into beautiful Val Fex. The hotel is strategically located for hiking—just outside the door, trails lead off in every direction:

up into the mountains, into the meadows, around the lakes, and along the rushing creek. This is a pretty inn and I love its comfortable ambiance with crisp white linens, fresh flowers, and endless thoughtful touches. It has an especially attractive, spacious dining room with windows overlooking the back garden with some lovely sitting places and a sheltered veranda. The dinner is a four-course menu and the food is excellent.

DESTINATION VIII   MÜSTAIR

Just a short distance traveling back up the valley from Sils Maria's peaceful, quiet setting is the very ritzy resort of **Saint Moritz**. Famous first as a health spa, Saint Moritz is now considered the playground of the wealthy. From there continue north following the Engadine Valley. You will pass through Zuoz, a small medieval village, along the way. Then head east from Zernez where the road travels through the heavily forested Swiss National Park, over the Ofenpass, and then down into the unspoiled rural beauty of the **Müstair Valley**.

Stretched along the sweep of the Müstair Valley are several unspoiled hamlets including **Santa Maria**, which appears at the bottom of the Ofenpass, and the village of **Müstair** just before the road crosses into Italy. This is a region of Switzerland that is almost Italian—the language and culture make it seem almost as if the border had slipped west to incorporate this pocket of Switzerland. We recommend here a very simple little inn— the **Chasa Chalavaina**, which has been restored with great respect for its past, with thick walls hung with farm instruments, doors with antique iron locks, old beams secured by wooden pegs, carved pine paneling wearing the patina of time, and rustic antiques galore. Delicious, home-cooked meals are served in the pine-paneled dining room. This is a marvelous value and makes for a delightful base from which to explore the Müstair Valley and for taking advantage of the many kilometers of unspoilt trails in the nearby **Swiss National Park**.

When it is time to leave Müstair, drive east for a few kilometers to where the Müstair Valley flows into Italy and then loops back across the Swiss border—following this suggested route saves backtracking along the same road. After crossing the border the route heads north just a few kilometers beyond customs and again across another border into Austria.

Shortly after entering Austria, the road travels back into the Engadine Valley and into Switzerland. This might sound confusing, but as you can see by the itinerary map, very few kilometers are actually involved and it is an easy trip. The other advantage to this route is that it travels near Samnaun, a town near the Austrian border, soon after reentering Switzerland. **Samnaun's** biggest attraction is its completely tax-free shopping. *Zoll Frei*, the prices are incredible and people come from all over to purchase Austrian and Swiss clothing, hiking equipment, and ski gear.

The final destination for this itinerary is in the Upper Engadine Valley. Driving the valley from the east, you will pass the famous spa town of Bad Scuol and then soon after the medieval town of **Guarda** appears perched on a ledge above the valley, very similar to Soglio. The views are spectacular and the opportunity exists for some marvelous walks. Superbly situated on its own terrace overlooking the valley and mountains sits one of our favorite places to stay, the **Hotel Meisser**—a beautiful hotel whose guestrooms in the main house are very reasonably priced. If you want to splurge, request a room across the street in the Chasa Pepina—the rooms are gorgeous and although more expensive, still an excellent value. Take advantage of the demi-pension rates and enjoy some excellent cuisine in the Meisser's most attractive dining room with its exceptional panoramas.

Tarasp Castle

The main recreation in Guarda is enjoying the stunning views or hiking along one of the many trails. However, if you want to explore, you will love the village of **Tarasp** and its picturesque castle, which are perched precariously on the opposite side of the valley, enjoying stunning mountain and valley views. If you venture here, there are endless trails, guided tours of **Tarasp Castle** in summer months, and another wonderful hotel, the **Schloss Hotel Chastè**. The Schloss Hotel Chastè has a marvelous restaurant and hikers seem content sitting on the terrace for a cold drink or delicious cakes and coffee. From this beautiful Engadine Valley, it is an easy half-day's drive either to Zürich or Lucerne.

Best on a Budget

Switzerland by Train, Boat & Bus

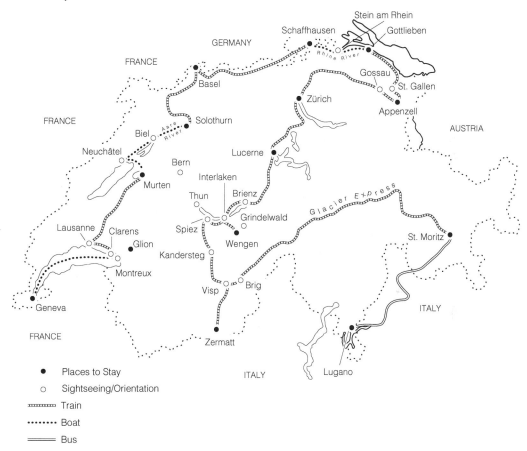

Stein am Rhein
Gottlieben
Schaffhausen
GERMANY
Rhine River
FRANCE
Basel
Gossau
St. Gallen
Zürich
Appenzell
FRANCE
Solothurn
AUSTRIA
Biel
Aare River
Neuchâtel
Lucerne
Bern
Murten
Interlaken
Glacier Express
Thun
Brienz
Lausanne
Clarens
Spiez
Grindelwald
Glion
Wengen
St. Moritz
Kandersteg
Montreux
Visp
Brig
Geneva
ITALY
FRANCE
Zermatt
Lugano
ITALY

● Places to Stay
○ Sightseeing/Orientation
▭▭▭ Train
•••••• Boat
═══ Bus

Switzerland by Train, Boat & Bus

Of all the itineraries in the guide, this is my favorite. It offers a variety of ways to travel from major cities to tiny hamlets via high mountain passes, lush valleys, lakes, and rivers—all without the use of a car. This is a long itinerary, so except for a few of you with the luxury of boundless time to spend, it should not be attempted in one trip: it would take too long—unless you rush from town to town, which you must not do. Therefore, read through the suggested routing carefully and choose the segment that appeals most to you, then go slowly. Savor each destination. Take time to enjoy the journey from place to place—your transportation becomes a major part of your holiday.

Travel at a leisurely pace. Relax and enjoy the incomparable beauty of Switzerland by train, boat, and bus.

The potential of this itinerary was realized while I was staying in Gottlieben, a town on the River Rhine. Noticing the ferry in front of the Hotel Krone departing to Schaffhausen, I wished I could just pick up my suitcase, climb on board and disembark a few hours later in front of another of my favorite hotels, the Rheinhotel Fischerzunft in Schaffhausen. How much more enjoyable to savor the lovely Rhine, passing along the way pretty little towns such as Stein am Rhein, rather than passing large trucks on a busy highway. The idea for this itinerary welled stronger a few days later when in Solothurn I was surprised to notice a boat connection to Murten, one of my favorite walled towns in Europe. How delightful, I thought, to journey through the countryside via canals and lakes instead of by car. So I returned home eager to see if the various travel segments by land and water could be coordinated. Knowing how remarkably efficient the Swiss transportation network is, I should never have doubted the feasibility of this itinerary. However, you will need to plan carefully as some of the ferries operate only from late spring to early autumn.

There are a few prerequisites to this style of travel. First, it is absolutely essential that you travel very lightly. If you feel you can't pack everything you need into one small suitcase, forget this itinerary. Cumbersome bags will be an aggravation, frustration, and burden when trying to make quick connections between trains or boats, which will certainly diminish some of the joy of travel. Secondly, it is *very* important that you buy one of the Swiss rail passes that are described in the introduction. I cannot overly stress the marvelous, carefree, total holiday feeling that comes from just hopping on and off trains, boats, and buses without any hassle of buying tickets. (There are a few trips such as the Glacier Express where reservations must be pre-booked, but these are rare.) Thirdly, buy the Official Timetable. This guide, published once a year, contains a wealth of information, outlining every timetable within Switzerland for boats, trains, buses, and even funiculars and cable cars. There are other train guides you can purchase, such as Cook's (see page 15), but this official guide is the only one we found that shows access

Switzerland by Train, Boat & Bus   101

by public transportation to every place in Switzerland—no matter how tiny or how isolated. It is unbelievably thorough. Once you get accustomed to using it, it will become your bible. You can purchase the Official Timetable in Switzerland at train stations or newsstands.

IMPORTANT NOTE: In this itinerary, suggested times are given for the trains, boats, and buses. These schedules are to be used as a guideline only. You **must** check each of the schedules locally to verify times of arrival and departure. Some trains, boats, and buses operate only on certain days of the week or during certain seasons of the year. Also, departure times can change. I debated whether or not to include the times and schedules, but decided that it was important to provide you with an approximate guideline so that you could see how the itinerary basically works and how it accommodates your own travel plans. However, it is terribly important to verify the schedules.

ORIGINATING CITY　　　　GENEVA

Geneva, the first city on this itinerary, is a delightful starting point for a Swiss vacation. Geneva is a lovely blend of the old and new, with the medieval portion of the city rising on the hillside on the left bank of the Rhône and the newer city stretching out with peaceful promenades on the right bank of the river. As you stroll the lake front of this international city, you will hear languages from all over the world and see costumes of many nations. In the spring Geneva becomes a small Holland, with glorious tulips blooming in every little park. The shopping in Geneva is wonderful—antique shops tempt the wallet in the old section and the most sophisticated shoppers can find their haven in the beautiful shops and arcades in the newer section.

DESTINATION I   GLION–MONTREUX or CLARENS

The journey from Geneva to Montreux is as much a sightseeing excursion as a means of transportation. This is a glorious outing taking you from the western end of **Lake Geneva** to the eastern tip, where you find the fashionable town of Montreux.

> 10:30 am depart Geneva (Jardin Anglais pier) by boat
> 3:42 pm arrive Territet (July 1–August 31 only) for Hotel Victoria

If you choose to stay at the Hotel Victoria, upon arrival in **Territet,** go straight ahead from the pier, following signs for the funicular that climbs up the hill to Glion. (It is about a two-minute walk from where the boat docks.) The funicular runs every 15 minutes on the quarter-hour, so you will not have long to wait. After a steep, short journey through the forest, you "land" at the Glion station and can see the Hotel Victoria, a French-looking château with mansard roof, on a knoll above and to the right of the station. It is a quick walk to the hotel. (If you have luggage, you can call the hotel and a porter will whisk down to assist you.)

Glion, a suburb of Montreux located high above the city, has spectacular views, which is probably why there are so many elegant villas tucked in the trees overlooking the lake. One of these, the **Hotel Victoria**, is set in its own exquisite gardens with a sweeping panorama of Lake Geneva. Staying at the Hotel Victoria you will feel like royalty. Almost all of the guestrooms have been renovated in the past few years and are beautifully decorated, each with its own personality. However, no matter how lovely the furnishings, nothing can compete with the magnificence of the view—for a memorable stay, request a room with a balcony overlooking the city of Montreux, Lake Geneva, and the distant Castle of Chillon off its shore. You might never want to wander from the front of the hotel with its lovely shade trees, velvety lawn, and perfectly tended beds of flowers. Here you can sit quietly on one of the strategically placed chairs and soak in the beauty of the lake whose deep-blue waters are enhanced by the magnificence of the majestic mountains that frame her southern shoreline.

Castle of Chillon, Lake Geneva

Switzerland by Train, Boat & Bus

DESTINATION II   MURTEN

Leaving Glion, your next destination is Murten. It is necessary to change trains twice, but the total travel time is short and the journey is beautiful.

9:43 am depart Glion by train
9:55 am arrive Montreux

10:10 am depart Montreux by train
10:31 am arrive Lausanne

11:29 am depart Lausanne by train
11:48 am arrive Murten

In **Murten**, we have three favorite hotels, **Le Vieux Manoir au Lac**, a charming country manor located just south of town on the lake at **Meyriez**, the **Hotel Schiff**, also located on the water's edge but just outside the gates of the walled city, and, in the heart of town, **Hotel Weisses Kreuz**. Whichever one you select will make a good base for exploring the quaint town of Murten. As you enter through the thick walls, you are magically transported back through the years to find yourself in one of the most romantic medieval villages in Switzerland. Murten is like a living museum—as you meander through the little streets, there are marvelous examples of medieval buildings, clock towers, ramparts, brightly painted fountains, and quaint little squares.

DESTINATION III   SOLOTHURN

Today's trip from Murten to Solothurn is similar to a treasure hunt as you weave your way by boat through the scenic lakes, canals, and rivers of the lovely Swiss countryside. Your adventure begins in the tiny walled village of Murten from where you take the ferry to Biel to board the boat for the final leg of your journey on the **River Aare** to the walled city of Solothurn.

I have already stressed that time schedules **must** be carefully checked. Of all the destinations, this one's schedule is the most important because the boats basically operate only in the summer and **not on Mondays**. However, if the boats do not operate to suit your time frame, it is always possible to make the journey from Murten to Solothurn by train. Another possibility: If you want to see the town of **Neuchâtel**, you can make this a luncheon stop en route to Biel if you leave Murten on an earlier boat.

11:40 am depart Murten by boat
 1:28 pm arrive Neuchâtel

2:05 pm depart Neuchâtel by boat
4:35 pm arrive Biel/Bienne

4:50 pm depart Biel/Bienne by boat
7:15 pm arrive Solothurn

Although it is not far from **Solothurn's** boat depot to your hotel, it will be a bit far to walk with luggage. If you ask in advance and advise them what time your boat is arriving, the Hotel Krone will send a taxi to the pier. Alternatively, when you dock, you can call for a cab. How very appropriate when in the ancient town of Solothurn to stay in an old inn that perpetuates the mood of antiquity. The location of the **Hotel Krone** is perfect and so easy to find—facing a little square opposite the impressive Saint Ursen Cathedral.

Solothurn is much larger than Murten, but also a marvelously preserved, completely walled medieval city located on the River Aare, so "perfect" that it was awarded the coveted Henry Louis-Wakker prize for excellence in renovation. Solothurn is one of the oldest Roman settlements in Switzerland. It is fascinating to walk through this ancient town so full of the colorful atmosphere of bygone years.

DESTINATION IV   BASEL

Your train journey today is short. You can plan for a leisurely morning departure and then still have the entire day to explore Basel.

10:15 am depart Solothurn by train
10:45 am arrive Moutier

10:49 am depart Moutier by train
11:38 am arrive Basel

There is such a famous hotel in **Basel** that it would be a shame to stay anywhere else. The **Hotel Drei Konige** is one of the oldest inns in Switzerland, dating from 1026. The hotel is also very historical, having been the site of the famous meeting of three kings (Conrad II, Henry III, and Rudolf III) who drew up the treaty for the transference of territories that are now western Switzerland and southern France. This historical meeting gave the hotel its name, which means "Three Kings."

The location of the Hotel Drei Konige on the River Rhine is terrific—not only can you enjoy watching the ever-changing drama of the river traffic passing by the hotel, but you are also only steps from the center of Basel. Although Basel is a large city, its heart is still a fun-filled medieval town of tiny squares, gay fountains, marvelously preserved old buildings, beautiful cathedrals, bridges, and many interesting museums.

DESTINATION V   SCHAFFHAUSEN

It is a simple and quick train ride from Basel to Schaffhausen, which allows time for another morning in Basel before continuing on to Schaffhausen.

1:05 pm depart Basel (Badischer Bahnhof) by train
3:18 pm arrive Schaffhausen

Munot Fortress at Schaffhausen on the Rhine

Schaffhausen, on the banks of the Rhine, is one of Switzerland's best-preserved medieval towns, with its many river jetties overshadowed by the circular keep of the Munot Fortress. Schaffhausen is a maze of alleys with clock towers, statues, and painted houses. Its name originates from the "ship houses" where cargo was stored when ships had to be unloaded for their goods to be carried past the falls and rapids. We recommend a hotel in Schaffhausen that is so delightful that the hotel would almost be worthy of a visit even if the town itself were not an attraction. The **Rheinhotel Fischerzunft** has an absolutely perfect location directly on the promenade on the banks of the Rhine.

Just a short drive west of Schaffhausen is the famous **Rheinfall** (Rhine Falls), which made it necessary for merchants to unload their river cargo and carry it around the falls before continuing their journey. (The town of Schaffhausen grew up to service this river commerce.) Whether you arrange for a car rental or taxi, be sure to go—this waterfall is the most dramatic in Europe. You can view the falls from the shore or you can take a tour on a little boat that maneuvers right up under the giant cascade of water.

DESTINATION VI   GOTTLIEBEN

This journey along the Rhine is wonderful, combining a splendid boat ride through quaint river villages with the practical aspect of traveling between two delightful hotels. You can select a direct ferry that takes about four hours or you can get off the ferry in the charming village of Stein am Rhein to have lunch before boarding the ferry again for the completion of your journey to Gottlieben.

9:10 am depart Schaffhausen by boat
11:10 am arrive Stein am Rhein

A luncheon stop is suggested in the picturesque medieval walled village of **Stein am Rhein**. Settle under an umbrella at one of the riverside restaurants, or park on a bench with a refreshing *apfelsaft, bratwurst, und brot* and enjoy the constant passage of boats that ply the river. Stein am Rhein, with its streets winding up from the river to the heart of the old town, is charming to explore on foot. Hauptstrasse and the Town Hall Square are extremely picturesque with their flower-decked fountains and oriel-windowed houses.

3:40 pm depart Stein am Rhein by boat
5:45 pm arrive Gottlieben

When you arrive at **Gottlieben** your hotel is conveniently located just a few steps from the pier. The **Hotel Krone** offers comfortable accommodation, a lovely indoor restaurant, and a café on the banks of the river for dining outside when days are warm.

It is necessary to take a ferry plus several trains between Gottlieben and Appenzell. It sounds complicated, but the Swiss in their predictable fashion have tailored the connections to work like a jigsaw puzzle—the connections fit together perfectly.

11:31 am depart Gottlieben by boat (July 14–September 8 only)
12:10 pm arrive Kreuzlingen

1:01 pm depart Kreuzlingen by train
1:26 pm arrive Romanshorn

1:34 pm depart Romanshorn by train
1:59 pm arrive Saint Gallen

2:37 pm depart Saint Gallen by train
3:21 pm arrive Appenzell

The decoratively painted **Hotel Säntis** and the **Hotel Appenzell** are located on a small square in the center of **Appenzell**. This village, a popular tourist destination because of its colorfully painted houses, is situated in a beautiful dairy-farm area of Switzerland with soft, rolling green hills dotted with farmhouses that are a combination of home and barn.

Hotel Appenzell, Appenzell

You can take a train from Appenzell to Zürich by making a connection in Gossau, but if the day is pleasant, it is more fun to combine your journey into a sightseeing excursion. This trip will include the great beauty of the verdant Appenzell rolling green hills, the charm of the medieval village of Rapperswil, and the fun of arriving in the city of Zürich by steamer.

10:01 am depart Appenzell by train
10:35 am arrive Herisau

11:10 am depart Herisau by train
11:56 am arrive Rapperswil

You can make a direct ferry connection from Herisau to Zürich, but a suggestion would be to lunch in the medieval town of **Rapperswil**. If time allows, visit the museum in the 13th-century massive **Rapperswil Castle** perched on a knoll just above the center of the town. This museum contains, among other artifacts, a fascinating collection of Polish treasures brought to Switzerland for protection during World War II.

1:45 pm depart Rapperswil by boat
3:40 pm arrive Zürich

In **Zürich**, it is approximately a ten-minute walk from the station along the *quai* to the **Hotel Zum Storchen** or just a few blocks farther along the cobbled streets to the **Hotel Kindli**. If you decide to stay at the very beautiful **Romantik Hotel Florhof** or the **Claridge Hotel Tiefenau**, it would be best to take a cab as they are a bit farther away and more difficult to find.

Although very popular with travelers from around the world, Zürich does not have the feeling of a tourist center. Instead, as you walk the streets, you feel the bustle of a "real" city. Of course there are tourists, but shopping next to you in the little boutique will be the local housewife, hurrying down the promenade are businessmen on their way to work, and a couple from Zürich will probably be sitting next to you at a sidewalk café. Nevertheless, there is a carnival atmosphere to Zürich, a gaiety to the city. From both sides of the river the old section of Zürich radiates out on little twisting streets like a spider web. Along the lake front are parks and gardens, and from the piers there is a fascinating variety of boat excursions to little villages around the lake. Since this is a large city, there is an excellent selection of museums to explore.

DESTINATION IX   LUCERNE

Lucerne

A constant "commuter" service exists between Zürich and **Lucerne** taking approximately an hour. The trains usually leave a minute after each hour. When you arrive in Lucerne, it is only a few minutes' taxi ride to one of our favorite Swiss hotels, the **Romantik Hotel Wilden Mann**. The location of the Wilden Mann Hotel is fabulous—on Bahnhofstrasse, in the middle of the old section of Lucerne within easy walking distance of all points of interest. The hotel embodies all that is best about Swiss hotels—the owner present to oversee every detail of management, excellent service from the staff, attractively decorated bedrooms, fine antiques liberally used in the public rooms, and a charming restaurant and intimate *stubli*.

Lucerne is a wonderful town for lingering: just strolling through the quaint streets and enjoying a snack in one of the small cafés overlooking the river can easily fill an afternoon. There are always many tourists—Lucerne's enchantment is no secret. Everyone seems happy and there is a holiday air to the city.

DESTINATION X   WENGEN

A frequent, direct train service runs from Lucerne to Interlaken, usually about every two hours. From there it is a beautiful short ride to Wengen.

1:54 pm depart Lucerne by train
3:59 pm arrive Interlaken Ost station

4:02 pm depart Interlaken Ost station by train
4:24 pm arrive Lauterbrunnen

4:35 pm depart Lauterbrunnen by train
4:49 pm arrive Wengen

I wish for you a clear day for this segment of your journey, truly one of spectacular beauty. First the train heads south from Lucerne, winding through gentle green valleys dotted with pretty farmhouses—a scene of rural beauty. From Interlaken, the train heads south to Lauterbrunnen where you change to a smaller train that chugs up a steep incline to **Wengen**, an idyllic small town clinging to a shelf perched high above the **Lauterbrunnen Valley**. Without a doubt, this is one of the most breathtaking settings in the world. As an added joy, there are no cars allowed in town—no pollution, no noise.

Our favorite places to stay in Wengen are the **Alpenrose**, the town's first hotel, and the **Hotel Regina**, an imposing Victorian building perched on a knoll overlooking the town. Neither the Alpenrose nor the Regina are pretentious, but each offers the warmth of family-owned establishments and has memorable views of the Jungfrau. (The other two peaks, the Eiger and the Mönch, must be viewed from a higher vantage point.)

Hotel Regina, Wengen

Wengen is a perfect starting point for the unforgettable **Jungfraujoch Excursion** — one you must not miss. This circular train trip, which winds its way through the meadows and then twists its way to the base of the Jungfrau, is one of the most dramatic rides in Switzerland.

From Wengen, it is easy to return to Interlaken where, just steps from the Ost station, you can climb aboard one of the ferry boats that makes its way along the river and on to Lake Brienz. A trip on this ferry with lunch at one of the small villages is highly recommended.

The **Open-Air Museum of Ballenberg** is an interesting sightseeing excursion from Wengen. Visiting Ballenberg is a wonderful way to learn about the various architectural styles and the crafts of Switzerland. This development reminds me of Rockefeller's preservation of the town of Williamsburg, reconstructing the style of living and crafts of the American heritage. Ballenberg is located in an enormous parklike setting in a meadow above Lake Brienz. Houses, grouped according to region, have been brought to the park to show the most important forms of housing and settlement. Crafts and old ways of living and working are demonstrated and the interiors of the houses offer a glimpse into yesterday with their antique furnishings. To reach Ballenberg from Interlaken, take the boat or train to Brienz, and from there take the bus to the park.

DESTINATION XI   ZERMATT

Your journey today will take you through some of the most spectacular mountain vistas in the world. This is an ideal trip by train since the section from Spiez to Brig takes the short cut through the Lotschberg Tunnel, which is restricted to train traffic. The final leg of your journey must be by train since cars are not allowed into Zermatt.

8:57 am depart Wengen by train
9:15 am arrive Lauterbrunnen

9:35 am depart Lauterbrunnen by train
9:57 am arrive Interlaken Ost

10:33 am depart Interlaken Ost by train
10:54 am arrive Spiez

10:58 am depart Spiez by train
12:03 pm arrive Brig

12:18 pm depart Brig by train
1:45 pm arrive Zermatt

There are no cars in **Zermatt**. However, when you arrive at the station, you will see waiting in the adjacent square electric carts or horses and buggies, sent from most of the hotels, waiting to pick up their guests. Zermatt has a rich selection of places to stay. We recommend several hotels in the heart of town—each has its own personality, each is quite delightful in its own way. Look in the hotel section to see which place seems to suit you best. The picturesque town of Zermatt has grown from a tiny farm community to a booming tourist destination. Condominiums dot the hillsides and new hotels are constantly under construction. However, there are strict building codes and fortunately the quaint nature of the town survives, watched over by the towering, oh-so-dramatic

Matterhorn. Best of all, Zermatt offers unparalleled walking and hiking possibilities. I'm sure you could stay a month, exploring new paths each day.

DESTINATION XII   SAINT MORITZ

Your trip between Zermatt and Saint Moritz is truly a dream come true for any train buff. It used to be that you had to hip-hop across Switzerland changing trains at various stations to travel between these two famous mountain towns, but a few years ago a resourceful Swiss entrepreneur connected the two towns by a private railroad, the enchanting **Glacier Express**. You board the little red train in the morning in Zermatt and pull into Saint Moritz station eight hours later. It is necessary to make reservations in advance for this train—contact Rail Europe through our website, *www.karenbrown.com*. The Glacier Express chugs over some of the highest Alpine passes in Switzerland, crosses meadows, tunnels through mountains, traverses glaciers, and weaves through canyons, all while you relax at your picture window. There is even more to the adventure if you plan ahead and make a luncheon reservation at the same time you book the train. If so, you have the pleasure of dining in an old-fashioned dining car brimming with nostalgia—wood-paneled walls, bronze fixtures, and tables set with crisp linens and fresh flowers. The train is expensive, but the journey is a train trip of a lifetime.

> 10:18 am depart Zermatt via the Glacier Express
> 6:10 pm arrive Saint Moritz

Upon arrival in **Saint Moritz**, there are many hotel possibilities. Look in the hotel section for the descriptions of our favorites: the **Hotel Eden**, the **Hotel Languard**, and the **Meierei Landhotel**. If you prefer a quiet location, you might choose the Meierei Landhotel, which is a bit out of town with a pretty setting on the lake and a view back to Saint Moritz. The Eden and the Languard are located in the center of town, more convenient to the train station and close to the boutiques.

The Swiss offer an intriguing list of possibilities for bus travel, giving some of the more popular routes a special name. One of these is called the **Palm Express**, which makes a one-day scenic journey from Saint Moritz to Lugano by bus and which we use for this itinerary. Note: Reservations are mandatory for the Palm Express. You can make these through your travel agent before leaving home, or else by calling the Palm Express office in Lugano: tel: (091) 807 85 20, fax: (091) 923 69 39, or in Saint Moritz: tel: (081) 837 67 64, fax: (081) 837 67 60.

> 12:10 pm depart Saint Moritz train station by bus
> 4:25 pm arrive Lugano train station

The bus heads south from Saint Moritz, passing by the pretty little Silvaplana and Silser lakes, then crosses over the twisting Malojapass and drops down to the beautiful Bregaglia Valley. The road passes through a bit of Italy before crossing back across the border again and on to Lugano. The bus arrives at the **Lugano** train station. Across from the train station, you can take a funicular down the hill and get off just a short walk from the **Romantik Hotel Ticino**. The Ticino, once a convent long ago, is located on the tiny Piazza Cioccaro in the old section of Lugano. It is a pretty hotel, filled with old-world character and enhanced by the graciousness of its owners, Claire and Samuel Buchmann.

Lugano is a delightful city. Although it has grown tremendously, its core still has the atmosphere of a small medieval village. From Lugano you can either continue on into Italy for further adventures or, if you want to complete your "Swiss Circle," there is frequent direct train service to Zürich taking only about three hours.

Swiss Highlights

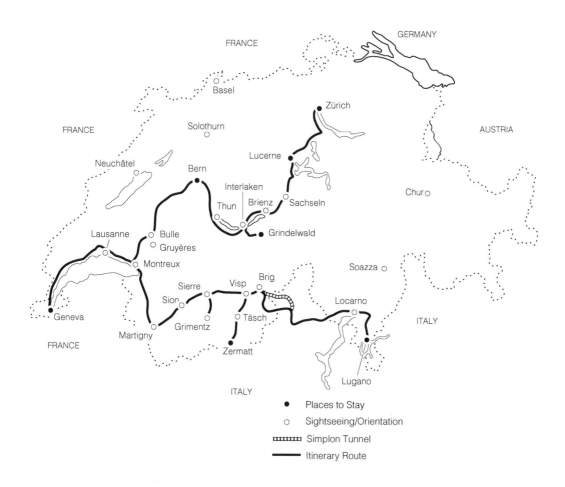

FRANCE

GERMANY

FRANCE

AUSTRIA

○ Basel

Solothurn
○

● Zürich

Neuchâtel
○

Bern
●

Lucerne ○

Chur ○

Interlaken

Thun ○   Brienz ○ Sachseln

○ Grindelwald ●

Lausanne
○   Bulle ○
○ Gruyères

Soazza ○

Montreux ○

○ Sierre   Visp   Brig
Sion ○   ○   ○
● Geneva   Martigny ●   Grimentz ○   Täsch ○

Locarno ○

ITALY

FRANCE

Zermatt ●

Lugano ●

ITALY

●	Places to Stay
○	Sightseeing/Orientation
▥▥▥	Simplon Tunnel
▬▬	Itinerary Route

119

Swiss Highlights

Cobbled Square of Gruyères

For the traveler who wants to see the highlights of Switzerland including the picture-book-perfect destinations repeatedly seen on postcards and read about in books, this is an ideal itinerary. The following path leads you through some of the most scenic areas of Switzerland and introduces you to a wonderful variety of famous cities, charming villages, beautiful lakes, lush valleys, and splendid mountains. The towns and destinations featured deserve the accolades of loyal tourists who return year after year to savor Switzerland's stunning scenery. If you have only a few days, you can take segments of this itinerary. As an example, you could take only the Zürich to Geneva portion. If you have already, on previous holidays, enjoyed Zürich, Lucerne, and Interlaken (one of the most famous trios), you could begin this itinerary in Geneva and end it in the Swiss-Italian Lake District. If your time is extremely limited, you could very easily journey from Zürich to Geneva in one day and even have time to squeeze in sightseeing along the way. This itinerary provides a framework to piece together your own custom tour of Switzerland's highlights.

ORIGINATING CITY   ZÜRICH

If you arrive by plane, the Zürich airport is an excellent introduction to marvelous Swiss efficiency. As in all countries, you must identify and collect your luggage, but once that task is accomplished, the Swiss have managed to eliminate most of the hassle and have conscientiously made life as simple as possible for the traveler. There is no need to bother with porters or suffer the burden of economizing by dragging your bags along at your side, as there are usually plenty of luggage carts neatly lined up ready for your free use. After loading your baggage on a cart, you do not have to go through any luggage inspection unless you have something to declare. Once through the baggage area, everything is well marked. If you need to make a hotel reservation, there is a desk set up for this purpose. If you want a car rental, this too is well marked. For those who want to take the train into either Zürich or direct to many of the other towns in Switzerland, the train station (*bahnhof*) is located on the lower level. There is a train information booth just to the left as you exit customs and a counter where, for a minimal charge, you can check your baggage directly from the airport to almost any train or bus station in Switzerland. There are also many shops, a post office, and banks, all efficiently set up and identified. When I first came out of the customs area, pulling my luggage cart, I was concerned to notice the arrows for the train station pointing down the escalator. Again, no problem. The Swiss have thought of everything: there are directions on each luggage cart showing how to take it on the escalator with you. You can take your cart all the way to the train or, if renting a car, directly to your car.

Taking the train into Zürich is really the quickest and most efficient means of transportation unless you have several people in your party, in which case a cab might prove economical and preferable.

For your first night in Switzerland, **Zürich** offers a rich selection of places to stay. One of our favorites is the **Hotel Zum Storchen** . This is not a simple country inn, but rather a sophisticated hotel with all the amenities a large city hotel has to offer. For all the Zum Storchen's modern improvements, it maintains the charm of one of the oldest hotels in Switzerland. The location is excellent, too—in the center of Zürich directly on the banks of the River Limmat just a few minutes' walk from where it flows into Lake Zürich. In the heart of the old quarter, the **Hotel Kindli** is a smaller hotel and a little less expensive. In a more residential area, but within walking distance of the old town, are two hotels that we also recommend: the charming **Claridge Hotel Tiefenau** and the beautifully refurbished **Romantik Hotel Florhof**.

DESTINATION I — LUCERNE

Even if you are planning your holiday as a driving vacation, refrain from picking up your car until you are ready to leave **Lucerne**. The roads are very congested between Zürich and Lucerne and there is no freeway linking them. Once you arrive in either city, there is no need for a car—actually, a car becomes somewhat of a nuisance. Walking is one of the major attractions of both cities, so, in this particular itinerary, I suggest you take the train from Zürich to Lucerne. There are trains constantly traveling between the two, and it is a most pleasant journey, taking just about an hour.

In Lucerne, the **Romantik Hotel Wilden Mann** is a perfect inn within a city. Rarely do you find a hotel, except in the countryside, that retains such a cozy, intimate feeling.

En route for Grindelwald, head south from Lucerne toward Hergswil. Near Stansstad follow the highway signs south toward Brienz. About midway between Lucerne and Brienz you pass through the town of **Sachseln** located on **Lake Sarner**. Take a few minutes to stop in Sachseln where you find in the center of town the church that is a very important for Swiss Catholics. Within the nave are the remains of **Saint Nicholas of Flüe** who is not only a religious hero, but also a patriotic hero of the Swiss. Saint Nicholas, a peasant with a reputation as a fair and peace-loving man, gained fame in the 15th century when he is credited with keeping peace within Switzerland and furthering the growth of the confederation. When disagreement threatened war between the cantons, parish priests went to consult Nicholas, who negotiated a compromise—instead of battling, Solothurn and Fribourg joined the confederation in 1481.

Leaving Sachseln, you pass through the little towns of Giswil, Daiserbuhl, and Lungern before going over the Brunig Pass. The road leads downward from the Brunig Pass to the town of Brienz. **Brienz**, beautifully situated on the lake, is a very popular resort and also one of Switzerland's wood-carving centers. On the outskirts of Brienz, located by the **Wyssensee**, **Ballenberg** is a marvelous open-air museum that serves as a wonderful introduction to the regional architecture and cultures of Switzerland. Historic buildings slated for destruction were saved, relocated, and restored to their original and authentic state. A path weaves through this park of over 80 hectares and travels a course that takes you through the various cantons of Switzerland. You can tour the park on foot or, for a fee, by horse and buggy. Due to the vastness of the park, even if you decide to selectively visit just a few cantons, plan on allocating at least a half day here.

Continuing on from Brienz, the drive along the north side of **Lake Brienz** is beautiful, with lovely views as you pass through the little towns of Oberried, Niederried, and Ringgenberg before arriving at Interlaken.

Open-Air Museum at Ballenberg

Interlaken (the name means "between lakes") is situated on a neck of land joining Lake Brienz with **Lake Thun**. The location is fabulous, with the two gorgeous lakes stretching out on each side of the town, plus excellent views of the **Jungfrau**. Understandably, the town has been a center of tourism for years. There are many large Victorian-style hotels, appealing shops, and inviting cafés lining the streets. Although Interlaken is a bit touristy, you can never dispute its spectacular location nor deny that Interlaken is a convenient stopover for the circle trip by rail to see the Jungfrau. However, our suggested alternative to staying in Interlaken is to continue just a short drive beyond Interlaken to Grindelwald where the mountains are right at your fingertips. Leaving Interlaken in the direction of Lauterbrunnen, you soon come to a split in the road. Turn left at this junction, following the road upward as it climbs toward the town of Grindelwald.

Grindelwald is the closest mountain village to the Jungfrau to which you can drive. The setting of this glacier village is spectacular, with views of three giant mountain peaks, the **Eiger**, the **Mettenberg**, and the **Wetterhorn**. Grindelwald serves as a perfect gateway for the train ride up to the base of the Jungfrau and is also a haven for hikers and climbers. In Grindelwald, we recommend two lovely small hotels, the **Fiescherblick** and the **Gletschergarten**. Read what we have to say about both in the hotel section—you can't go wrong with either of them.

Allow two nights in Grindelwald, for you will need most of one day for the Jungfraujoch excursion. Allow more days if you also want to enjoy the beauty of the mountains. Grindelwald is an ideal place for either strenuous mountain climbing or leisurely walks along gentle trails.

DESTINATION III   BERN

From Grindelwald return to Interlaken and then take the highway marked to Thun. If you have allocated the whole day to sightseeing, a stop at **Thun**, located at the west end of Lake Thun, would prove the ideal spot for lunch. Thun is a picturesque medieval village with a castle crowning the hillside. From the turrets of the castle, now open to the public as a museum, you can enjoy a beautiful panorama of Thun, the lake, and mountains beyond. Getting to the castle is fun because the pathway up from the village is via a covered staircase.

Leaving Thun, stay on the freeway to Bern. It is only a short drive and the faster road will afford more time for sightseeing. Another of Switzerland's beautifully preserved medieval towns, **Bern** is nestled in a loop of the **River Aare** at a point where its banks fall steeply to the river below. To further enhance the setting, the Alps rise in the background. The setting alone would make Bern worth a stop, but the town itself is brimming with character—truly a storybook 13th-century wonderland, the only Swiss city that has been declared a world heritage landmark. The whole town seems to have a festive air—from its comical fountains to its jolly clock tower. Situated at the edge of the intriguing old sector of the city is the elegant **Gauer Hotel Schweizerhof**. With such an excellent location, this is an ideal base from which to explore Bern on foot. From the Schweizerhof you can walk to most of the tourist attractions or wander along the arcaded sidewalks. A less expensive choice, also centrally located, is the **Hotel Belle Époque,** a comely small hotel with art-nouveau décor, while the **Innere Enge** is the place to stay for jazz fans.

The River Aare and the Skyline of Bern

Leaving Bern, it is just a short drive south to the town of **Fribourg**, located on the banks of the **River Sarine**. Fribourg is a beautifully preserved medieval city with a town hall, Cathedral of Saint Nicholas, clock tower, and Church of Notre Dame.

Gruyères is located only a few kilometers off the freeway running south from Fribourg. After leaving Fribourg, you soon see signs to Bulle and Gruyères at which point you leave the freeway. After passing through the town of Bulle you will soon spot **Gruyères** crowning the top of a small hill. This village is actually one main street of beautifully preserved buildings at the end of which is a castle, open to the public daily during summer. Gruyères is so wonderful that it is considered a national monument. You cannot drive your car here, but parking is provided below the village. Gruyères attracts so many tourists that its charm is marred somewhat by mobs of people during the tourist season. However, with such beautiful views of lush green meadows and towering mountains, it is certainly worth a detour. Another plus—this is the heart of Switzerland's dairy area: stop for a famous Gruyères quiche.

Leaving Gruyères, return again to the highway and continue south to Vevey. From Vevey, take the freeway west toward Geneva. An alternative to the freeway would be to travel the lakeside road dotted with many charming waterfront towns.

Geneva is a lovely city graced by French influence. Geneva is frequently thought of as a "new" city—a city of banking and commerce, an international city housing the Palais des Nations, a sophisticated city of beautiful shops, a cultural city with many museums, an industrial city. All this is true, but Geneva also contains one of the most attractive "old towns" in Switzerland: on the south side of the River Rhône the hills rise steeply and twist and turn in a maze of little shops, fountains, flowers, and charming buildings. This area is crowned by Saint Peter's Cathedral.

Geneva is home to a string of majestic hotels that line the lake. If you prefer to be in the old quarter of Geneva, **Hotel les Armures** has character and charm. Within walking distance of the water and the old quarter is a lovely, elegant hotel, **La Cigogne**, and her neighboring, sister property, the **Hotel Touring-Balance**.

DESTINATION V   ZERMATT

Leaving Geneva, retrace your route along the north shore of **Lake Geneva**. The way has two choices: either a fast freeway or a much slower country road that traces the lake's shore, meandering through the quaint towns lining the lake. Mountains enclose both sides of the valley and on the lower hills, terraced to the water's edge, stretch the acres and acres of vineyards that make this region so well known—the vineyards and the small villages make a beautiful drive. Allow yourself enough time to follow roads that wind down to the villages on the lake and sample some of the region's wonderful wine.

At the east end of Lake Geneva, take a short detour to visit the **Castle of Chillon**, dramatically perched on its own little peninsula jutting into the lake. After visiting the castle, return to the freeway and continue following the River Rhône as it winds its way down the flat valley. The section of the Rhône Valley between Lake Geneva and the Zermatt turnoff is pretty, but does not have the pristine beauty found so frequently in other Swiss valleys—the road passes through many industrial areas. However, there are countless side valleys and intriguing passes to explore.

Many of these side valleys (accessible by narrow twisting roads) are well worth a detour if you have the time. A favorite is a pass climbing up to the tiny village of Grimentz. The turnoff for Grimentz is near the city of Sierre. At Sierre, watch carefully for signs for the road that runs to the south of the highway and direct you on to Grimentz.

Vineyards along the Shore of Lake Geneva

The small mountain village of **Grimentz** is an architectural gem and is protected by the Swiss government. The steep, narrow, curving access road to Grimentz is physically demanding, so don't attempt this side trip in the winter, but in the summer, if the day is clear and you are not intimidated by mountain driving, Grimentz makes a rewarding detour. This very old village is filled with marvelously preserved Valais-style homes whose heavy slate roofs are weighted down by chunky rocks to protect them against the winter storms. Park your car at the entrance to the village and stroll down the tiny streets that are closed to all but foot traffic. The lanes are lined by simple wood houses whose rough-hewn, age-blackened exteriors contrast dramatically with masses of flowers cascading from every windowbox. It is hard to believe that the Grimentz of old could ever have been as picturesque as it is today, for each resident seems to vie with his neighbor for the most stunning display of brilliant red geraniums. The effect captivates the senses: brilliant blue sky (with a little luck), snow-capped mountains, green pastures, characterful wooden houses, and flowers, flowers, flowers. If the timing is right, after wandering through the village, stop for a cheese fondue lunch at the **Hotel de Moiry**.

After the side trip to Grimentz, return to the freeway and continue east. As you near Visp, take the well-marked turnoff south toward Zermatt. The only choice you have along the way is where the road splits: the left branch of the road leads to Saas-Fee and the right leads to Zermatt.

You cannot drive into **Zermatt** as no cars are allowed within the city limits. However, this is not a problem as there are car parks at each of the small neighboring towns. **Täsch** is as far as you can go by car, so park here, buy your ticket at the small station, and board the train for the rest of your journey. After only a few minutes' ride you arrive at the Zermatt train station where you will notice horse-drawn carriages waiting in the plaza in front of the station. In winter, these convert to horse-drawn sleighs. In the past few years, electric golf-type carts have gradually replaced some of the horses and sleighs. Most of the major hotels will send their "carriage" to meet the incoming train—each hotel has its name on the cart or carriage or the porter's cap. If for some reason you do not see "your" porter, you will find many electric taxis also available or you can call the hotel from one of the telephone booths next to the station.

Zermatt offers many places to stay. A favorite, the **Romantik Hotel Julen**, is located just beyond Zermatt's city center so you feel you are somewhat away from the tourist bustle. The hotel has an inviting old-world charm, with a cozy fireplace in the reception hall, antiques artfully arranged throughout, an attractive restaurant, and a cheerful little patio in the rear. If you are very lucky, you might even be able to snare one of the bedrooms from which you can watch the various moods of the majestic Matterhorn.

First you need to return by train from Zermatt to Täsch pick up your car for the long day's drive from Zermatt to the Swiss-Italian Lake District—try for an early departure. Head north to Visp where you join the N9 freeway going in the direction of Brig.

If you want to include a little sightseeing on the way to Brig, stop to visit **Stockalperschloss**, one of the most interesting castles in Switzerland. Built in the 17th century by a very wealthy merchant, Kaspar Jodok Stockalper Von Thurm, this castle was the largest private residence in Switzerland and is now open to the public, May to October, from 9 to 11 am and from 2 to 5 pm. The castle is closed on Mondays. Thereare frequent guided tours taking about 45 minutes.

Ascona on Lake Maggiore

The N9 heads southeast after Brig to take you over the **Simplon Pass** into Italy. The first small town across the border is Iselle, then you come to the town of Crevoladossola and, only a few minutes further on, to Domodossola. There are signs at Crevoladossola to direct you left along a road to Locarno. This is a short cut to the Swiss-Italian lakes, truly a spectacular drive following a river gorge but frankly, it is a very narrow road and a bit treacherous, so you may want to stay on the main highway and head south toward Verbania and then follow **Lake Maggiore** north toward Locarno. Before reaching Locarno, you come to the little town of **Ascona** nestled at the northern end of the lake. This would be a good place to lunch or have a cup of coffee. There are many street cafés that overlook the lake. My favorite is the café in front of the **Hotel Tamaro**. After a break for a snack and perhaps a little shopping spree on one of the ancient little streets branching out behind the lakefront, continue on through Locarno and from there to Bellinzona where you join the freeway heading south to Lugano.

Lugano has a complicated street plan and it is difficult to find and maneuver your way to the heart of the old section. Be sure to have a good map and patience—even though you can pinpoint on the map where you want to go, it is not easy. You might have to make several loops about the old town on one-way streets until you finally succeed in entering the old section. Take heart—it is worth the effort. The outskirts of Lugano make up an unattractive large metropolis, but once you are in the heart of the city you will discover a real gem, the Lugano of old.

Tucked away in this atmospheric section of Lugano is the delightful **Romantik Hotel Ticino**. Fronting a small square, the Piazza Cioccaro, the Ticino is tiny but full of charm. The Piazza Cioccaro is closed to cars, but if you are a guest at the Ticino, you can pass the barricades and drive to the entrance of the hotel to leave your luggage. When you check in, the receptionist will tell you where you can park your car. To the right of the reception area is a small dining room—intimate and attractive. Beyond the reception desk, stairs lead to the upper floors where the bedrooms and lounges are located. A central patio is a reminder of long ago when the hotel was a convent.

Lugano is a wonderful small city to linger in. The ambiance is more Italian than Swiss— not surprising since you are almost on the Italian border. The old section of town is wonderful for browsing and the lakeside promenade a delight for lazy strolling.

Most fun of all, there is a wonderful selection of boats waiting at the pier to take you to beckoning little towns snuggled along the shores of the lake. From Lugano, you can cross into Italy where it is an easy drive to the international airport of Milan, or you can head north again into the Alps and complete a circle back to Zürich.

The River Limmat, Zürich

134

Hotel Descriptions

If you dream of staying in a tiny, romantic hideaway, tucked high on a splendid mountain meadow with incredible views, look no further. La Renardière captures all the magic of Heidi's Switzerland, plus much more. This is the Swiss setting we had always hoped to discover, but which had always eluded us. A tiny lane winding up through untouched gorgeous mountain scenery leads you to La Renardière, a captivating, 200-year-old stucco-and-wood farmhouse enhanced by red geraniums in flowerboxes. This is the home of your charming hostess, Nicole Ferreux. A French chef prepares a delicious dinner, which is served in a cozy niche in front of a blazing fire. When the evening is balmy, meals are served outside or, for a larger group, in the adjacent, totally delightful stables. This building also contains one lovely suite. Nearby in a converted barn there are two more guestrooms and a sitting room with kitchen, all of which can be converted into a marvelous apartment. La Renardière is a fabulous gem for anyone looking for a simple, secluded, tiny inn with a stunning location, fabulous food, and a wonderful hostess. Note: La Renardière is a private club, so mention that you were recommended by Karen Brown. *Directions:* From Gruyères take road 12 for about 9 km to Albeuve. Turn right onto Route des Prés d'Albeuve. Go up the hill and at the first junction, keep right. At the next junction, turn left. La Renardière is the last farmhouse on your left.

LA RENARDIÈRE
Owner: Nicole Ferreux
Route des Prés d'Albeuve
CH-1669 Albeuve–Les Prés d'Albeuve, Switzerland
Tel & fax: (026) 928 28 02
3 rooms, Double: CHF 280–CHF 330*
*Includes breakfast & dinner
Open: all year
9 km S of Gruyères, Train: 5 km (in Albeuve)
Region: Fribourg
karenbrown.com/switzerland/renardiere.html

On my first visit to the Hotel Stern and Post my heart was won by Faro, an enormous Bernese farm dog napping in the middle of the lobby. Faro was such a fixture that postcards of this gentle "puppy" were sent to his many admirers. Unfortunately Faro has died, but Duke, an equally lovable Bernese farm dog is now winning the hearts of guests. The Stern and Post has been in the Tresch family for several hundred years. Elisabeth Tresch, who graduated from Cornell University Hotel School in New York, oversees the hotel with an unparalleled professionalism and warmly welcomes guests from all over the world. Her family heirlooms adorn the cozy, antique-adorned public areas and a wonderful story can be told about each—ask about the veterinary cabinet or the lock-up cabinet for the hotel silver, necessary in days of old when the employees were not to be trusted. Right on the main thoroughfare of Amsteg, the oldest part of the house dates back to 1789 when the inn was built to provide shelter to weary travelers. Today the Stern and Post is the only remaining coaching station along the Saint Gotthard Pass road. About a third of the simple guestrooms have antique furnishings, others have a modern decor. Ask for one of the bedrooms in the back overlooking the gushing stream. *Directions:* Take the Amsteg exit from the A2. The hotel is at the center of the village, approximately .5 km from the exit.

HOTEL STERN AND POST
Owner: Elisabeth A. Tresch
Gotthardstrasse 88
CH-6474 Amsteg, Switzerland
Tel: (041) 883 14 40, Fax: (041) 883 02 61
24 rooms, Double: CHF 175–CHF 250
Open: all year, Credit cards: all major
14 km S of Altdorf, Train: 6.5 km
Region: Uri
karenbrown.com/switzerland/hotelsternandpost.html

The attractive town of Appenzell with its cobbled streets and bounty of shops is at the heart of the canton that bears the same name. At the edge of the pedestrian district on the historic Landgemeindeplatz, the Hotel Appenzell benefits from the expertise and warmth of the Sutter family who own it. Margrit is often present to greet guests at the front desk, while Leo is responsible for the restaurant's fine offerings. The hotel has 16 lovely guestrooms, all with private bathroom and either tub or shower. The hallways leading to the guestrooms are uncluttered and attractive with a few well-placed antiques. The rooms, whose doors are adorned with lovely stenciling, are similar in their decor and differ only in their color scheme—a soft yellow for the first-floor rooms and a soft rose for the second-floor accommodations. The guestrooms are new, and tastefully and comfortably appointed. The restaurant is always bustling either with lunch or dinner guests, or, between meals, with those who are tempted by pastries from the adjacent bakery. A standard dinner menu offers traditional Swiss fare at a reasonable price. A breakfast buffet for hotel guests is offered in the intimate Dr Hildebrand Suite. *Directions:* Traveling from Zürich, take the Winkeln/Appenzellerland exit. Follow signposts for Herisau/Appenzell. At the roundabout, turn right. After 400 meters you'll find the Landgemeindeplatz, where you can park briefly in front of the hotel.

HOTEL APPENZELL
Owners: Margrit & Leo Sutter
Am Landgemeindeplatz
CH-9050 Appenzell, Switzerland
Tel: (071) 788 15 15, Fax: (071) 788 15 51
16 rooms, Double: CHF 186–CHF 210
Closed: Nov, Credit cards: all major
20 km S of St. Gallen, Train: 400 meters
Region: Appenzell, Interior Rhodes
karenbrown.com/switzerland/hotelappenzell.html

The façade of the Romantik Hotel Säntis, located on the central square in the picturesque village of Appenzell, has been gaily painted a rust-red with yellow and black scrolling. The terrace in front is a favorite place for a cool drink on a warm day. Guestrooms are decorated either in attractive modern or reproduction country-style wooden furniture. The price for the room depends mostly upon its size. My favorite guestrooms are in the original part of the main house, although those in the newer wing are also very pleasant. The decor of each bedroom in the new wing is the same except for the color scheme. The public rooms seem geared to the influx of tourists who drop in for a midday meal, but the lobby offers a country welcome, and the hotel has wisely insulated a quiet, peaceful lounge just for guests. A wing opened in 1997 houses a sauna, wellness bar, seminar center, and five additional large bedrooms. The gracious Stefan and his delightful Scottish wife, Catriona, are the fourth generation of the Heeb family to run the hotel and the family's pride and dedication as owners are very apparent, from the friendliness of the front-desk receptionist to the smile of the chambermaid. *Directions:* Traveling from Zürich, take the Winkeln/Appenzellerland exit. Follow signposts for Herisau/Appenzell. At the roundabout, turn right. After 400 meters you'll find the Landgemeindeplazt, where you can park briefly in front of the hotel.

ROMANTIK HOTEL SÄNTIS
Owners: Stefan A. & Catriona Heeb family
CH-9050 Appenzell, Switzerland
Tel: (071) 788 11 11, Fax: (071) 788 11 10
37 rooms, Double: CHF 110–CHF 150
Open: Feb to Dec, Credit cards: all major
20 km S of St. Gallen, Train: 400 meters
Region: Appenzell, Interior Rhodes
karenbrown.com/switzerland/romantikhotelsantis.html

One of Switzerland's most deluxe hotels and a member of Relais & Châteaux, the Castello del Sole is is a complete resort set in such a spectacular estate, with so many things to do, that you will be tempted not to leave the grounds. If you can afford to stay in one of the Pavilion suites, you may never leave your room—both breakfast and dinner can be served in your suite or on your balcony overlooking the estate (this wing of rooms is air-conditioned). If your budget precludes you from selecting the most expensive accommodation, do not worry, for all the rooms are lovely. While the hotel has an à-la-carte dining room, I suggest that you opt for either half board (lots of choices in each dinner course) or full board, which includes a wonderful luncheon buffet either in the garden, or in the restaurant when the weather is inclement. Get your exercise in the indoor/outdoor heated pool or on one of the seven tennis courts. Pamper yourself with facials and massages, enjoy the sauna, steam, and weight rooms, or simply stroll in the acres of grounds, perhaps taking the path down to the lake or visiting the hotel's vineyard. Practice on the putting green and enjoy a game at the adjacent golf course. A shuttle bus takes you into Ascona or you can borrow one of the hotel's bicycles. *Directions:* Arriving in Ascona, head for the town center—do not enter the pedestrian zone—and continue until you see the hotel's signposts directing you to the estate.

♨ ☕ ⚒ 🍲 CREDIT 📷 🏠 🛗 🚹 🏋 🎿 👪 🐎 🍸 P 🍴 🏊 🏃 🖼 ⛷ 🏄 🪑 🍇

CASTELLO DEL SOLE
Manager: Simon V. Jenny
Via Muraccio, 142
CH-6612 Ascona, Switzerland
Tel: (091) 791 02 02, Fax: (091) 792 11 18
83 rooms, Double: CHF 520–CHF 1500
Open: Mar 27 to Oct 24, Credit cards: all major
3 km SW of Locarno, Train to Locarno: 6 km
Relais & Châteaux
Region: Ticino
karenbrown.com/switzerland/castellodelsole.html

The Romantik Hotel Castello enjoys an imposing position at one end of Ascona's lakeside promenade. This 13th-century castle has been extended over the years but still keeps its fortress look with thick walls and stone stairways. Guestrooms with handsome wood doors are decorated with a mix of modern and traditional furnishings. The most impressive room is the tower room with its thick walls, high ceilings, and incredible frescoes. Guests who elect to stay on a demi-pension basis are offered an enticing menu served in a special dining room just for hotel guests. An à-la-carte restaurant, the Locanda de'Ghiriglioni, is also available for guests not opting for demi-pension and for non-residents. Tucked in the cellar, an attractive wine bar is a cozy place to enjoy a drink. Behind the castle is a secluded swimming pool and two wings of more contemporary bedrooms. Just across the road is an appealing, tree-shaded, lakeside garden where guests can relax while watching the colorful parade of people strolling along the promenade. *Directions:* Arriving in Ascona, follow signs for the town center and as you see the pedestrian zone ahead of you, follow signs for lake parking. As you come to the lake, the Hotel Castello is on your right. Pull into the driveway to unload then park in the hotel's underground car park.

ROMANTIK HOTEL CASTELLO-SEESCHLOSS
Owner: Werner Ris
Lakeside Promenade
CH-6612 Ascona, Switzerland
Tel: (091) 791 01 61, Fax: (091) 791 18 04
45 rooms, Double: CHF 248–CHF 548
Open: Mar to Nov, Credit cards: all major
3 km SW of Locarno, Train to Locarno: 6 km
Region: Ticino
karenbrown.com/switzerland/romantikcastello.html

Facing Lake Maggiore, Hotel Tamaro, a Ticino-style patrician house, is smartly attired in soft yellow with crisp-white shutters. Its tables and chairs spill out onto the lakeside promenade, creating a pleasing picture. Strollers settle here and enjoy a cup of coffee or an ice cream while leisurely watching the little ferryboats glide in and out. You may well be welcomed by Evelyn, the charming daughter of Annetta and Paolo Witzig, owners of the Tamaro. The hotel's inner courtyard (crowned by a glass ceiling for protection against inclement weather) has tables set gaily among many plants, giving the feeling that you are dining in a garden. The guestrooms are situated on various levels, and it's almost a game to find your room. Each bedroom varies greatly in style of decor, views, and size. I particularly enjoyed room 6, a standard corner room with windows facing both up the promenade and to the lake. The rooms are all decorated attractively with a charming, home-like ambiance throughout. Request a lake view—some even have a small balcony overlooking the promenade. *Directions:* In Ascona follow signs for the town center and as you see the pedestrian zone on the lakeside follow the waterfront to the hotel. You may drive up to the hotel to check in.

HOTEL TAMARO
Owners: Annetta & Paolo Witzig
Piazza G. Motta 35
CH-6612 Ascona, Switzerland
Tel: (091) 785 48 48, Fax: (091) 791 29 28
48 rooms, Double: CHF 190–CHF 290
Open: Mar to mid-Nov, Credit cards: all major
3 km SW of Locarno, Train to Locarno: 6 km
Region: Ticino
karenbrown.com/switzerland/hoteltamaro.html

The Hotel Drei Konige (Three Kings Hotel), the oldest hotel in Europe (1026), was originally called Zur Blume (At the Sign of the Flower). However, soon after the inn was founded, a historic meeting took place between three kings: Conrad II (Emperor of the Holy Roman Empire), his son (who became Henry III), and Rudolf III (King of Burgundy). At the meeting a treaty was drawn up for the transference of the territories that are now western Switzerland and southern France. The hotel's name was then changed, understandably, from Zur Blume to Drei Konige. The Drei Konige is decorated with exquisite taste—formal antiques and lovely reproductions are found in the public rooms and guestrooms. Many family oil paintings adorn the walls, creating a homey ambiance throughout the hotel. A sweeping staircase leading to the bedrooms opens to a central atrium. All of the bedrooms (even those in the standard category) are tastefully furnished. The rooms on the second or fourth floor that have a balcony overlooking the Rhine are truly superb. The suites also are spectacular, especially the Napoleon Suite, in regal shades of blue with an ornate ceiling—fit for a king. *Directions:* The Hotel Drei Konige is located on the road that follows the course of the river, just down from the Mittlere Rheinbrücke and near the Alte Universität.

HOTEL DREI KONIGE
Manager: Rudolph Schiesser
Blumenrain 8
CH-4001 Basel, Switzerland
Tel: (061) 260 50 50, Fax: (061) 260 50 60
88 rooms, Double: CHF 440–CHF 1800*
*Breakfast not included: CHF 32
Open: all year, Credit cards: all major
100 km N of Bern, Train: 1 km
Region: Basel
karenbrown.com/switzerland/dreikonige.html

If you are a fan of art nouveau, the Hotel Belle Époque, a boutique city hotel at the heart of this medieval city, is tailor-made for you. The hotel was renovated and refurnished in spring 2000 with a stylish and contemporary backdrop, done by one of Switzerland's finest interior decorators. Art nouveau (belle époque) furnishings and art from the early 1900s set the theme for the hotel—from the large paintings and murals in the cozy breakfast room and delightful bar, to the paintings hung in each of the bedrooms. The bedrooms are priced based on size. All have different color schemes that complement the artwork and lovely old furniture. Rooms with a view face the busy street while those at the back offer peace and quiet. Light refreshments are served in the bar and at the tables that form a terrace on the sidewalk under Bern's famous arcade—a delightful place to people watch. For dinner you can dine at the elegant in-house restaurant Le Chariot or have the friendly staff direct you to a restaurant in town. *Directions:* To find the hotel it is important that you exit the autobahn at Bern-Wankdorf and follow signs for zentrum. When you see the old town across the river turn over the bridge and the hotel is on your right after 50 meters. Unload in front of the hotel and you will be directed to parking.

HOTEL BELLE ÉPOQUE
Owners: Mr. Jürg and Mrs. Bice Musfeld-Brugnoli
Gerechtigkeitsgasse 18
CH-3011 Bern, Switzerland
Tel: (031) 311 43 36, Fax: (031) 311 39 36
17 rooms, Double: CHF 280–CHF 560*
*Breakfast not included: CHF 15
Open: all year, Credit cards: all major
In the old section of Bern, Train: 2 km
Region: Bern
karenbrown.com/switzerland/hotelbelleepoquesw.html

At the edge of the medieval city of Bern, just opposite the train station, is a beautiful city hotel whose name reflects the caring family behind its operations. The contents of the hotel constitute the largest private art and furniture collection in Bern. Although a new wing of 12 rooms has been added, the majority of rooms are housed in a building that dates back 142 years. A traditional decor has been selected for most of the guestrooms, so be sure to state a preference for traditional or modern when making a reservation. Even though the rooms at the front overlooking Bahnhofplatz are amazingly quiet behind double-paned windows, rooms at the back are assured of quiet even with the windows ajar. All of the rooms are air-conditioned. You can enjoy excellent food in Jack's Brasserie or intimate dining in one of the hotel's traditional dining rooms. The Schultheissenstube is Swiss-cozy, with a beamed ceiling and walls hung with tapestries, while the Simmentalerstube is housed in an old mountain chalet that has been relocated to the hotel. *Directions:* Arriving in Bern, follow signs for zentrum and bahnhof till you see the hotel opposite the train station.

GAUER HOTEL SCHWEIZERHOF
Manager: Paul B. Mattenberger
Bahnhofplatz 11
CH-3001 Bern, Switzerland
Tel: (031) 326 80 80, Fax: (031) 326 80 90
84 rooms, Double: CHF 415–CHF 1800
Open: all year, Credit cards: all major
In the heart of old Bern, Train: walking distance
Region: Bern
karenbrown.com/switzerland/schweizerhof.html

Just a bus ride away from Bern in a quiet residential suburb, the Innere Enge is the place to stay if you are a jazz fan like Hans Zurbrügg, the owner of the hotel. Soft music plays in the all the public rooms (even the bathrooms). Seven of the bedrooms are named after famous jazz musicians and contain memorabilia relating to that person's career. Downstairs is a jazz club where regular concerts are held (except in summer). Hans is the organizer of the Bern Jazz Festival, so a great many noted players play here. Whether or not you decide to stay in a "theme" room, you will be very happy with the room's size and pleasing contemporary decor. A fire burns in the entrance hall in the winter, providing a cozy place to settle, while in summer guests usually congregate on the terrace under the sycamore trees. The delightful brasserie serves a morning breakfast buffet, lunch, dinner, and afternoon tea. The Innere Enge has been an excursion destination since the early 18th century: eminent visitors include Napoleon's wife, the Empress Josephine. On a clear winter's day you can enjoy views from the garden across the city skyline to the distant Alps. *Directions:* Exit the autobahn at Bern-Neufeld and follow zentrum signs for 1 km to the traffic circle where you turn left on the Engerstrasse. The hotel is on your right after 500 meters.

INNERE ENGE
Owners: Hans Zurbrügg & Marianne Gauer
Engerstrasse 45
CH-3012 Bern, Switzerland
Tel: (031) 309 61 11, Fax: (031) 309 61 12
26 rooms, Double: CHF 250–CHF 830
Open: all year, Credit cards: all major
On the outskirts of Bern, Train: 5 minutes by bus
Region: Bern
karenbrown.com/switzerland/innereenge.html

Windowboxes hung heavy with geraniums color the wonderful weathered façade of the Chalet Schönegg. With views looking out over Brienz and across the lake to the majestic peaks beyond, this charming country hotel enjoys a lovely, peaceful setting. Guestrooms are housed in three buildings, the Schönegg, Chalet, and Spycher. A wonderful wooden free-standing chalet-cottage dating back to 1602, the Spycher houses three rooms that are gems: rooms 61, 62, and 63. Rooms 62 and 63 are found on the second floor, tucked under beamed ceilings, with wood-paneled walls, sitting areas, and views out through low windows to the lake. Room 62, a personal favorite, has Swiss farm-style painted furnishings and cozy fabrics selected for the drapes and comforter covers. Each room has a private bath. Room 61, a garden-level room in the same little chalet, is also charming, but not quite as cozy since it does not have the angled ceilings. In both the main house, the Schönegg, and the neighboring Chalet, guestrooms are more motel-like in style and furnishings. They are, however, quiet and enjoy wonderful views. Breakfast is offered in the main house, and a sitting area off the breakfast area is a friendly place to gather, particularly when the fire is lit. A grassy terrace off the salon is a peaceful spot to enjoy a lazy afternoon. *Directions:* Located on the hillside above the heart of town. Watch for signs from the road directing you to the hotel.

CHALET HOTELS SCHÖNEGG & SPYCHER GARNI
Owner: Christine Mathyer
Talstrasse 8
CH-3855 Brienz, Switzerland
Tel: (033) 951 11 13, Fax: (033) 951 38 13
16 rooms, Double: CHF 130–CHF 185
Open: Apr to Oct, Credit cards: MC, VS
18 km W of Interlaken, Train: 500 meters
Region: Bern
karenbrown.com/switzerland/chalethotels.html

The Hostellerie Lindenhof has an absolutely gorgeous setting above Brienz on an expanse of grounds and beautiful gardens. Housed in five separate buildings, guestrooms vary dramatically—from standard to "adventure" rooms. Adventure rooms are a bit more eccentric in decor, the Heustock and Touristorama being two fun examples. The Heustock (Haystack) room has pine beds covered with red-check comforters and enjoys a view across a private terrace to the surrounding greenery. A loft is filled with hay for a sense of adventure. Referred to by the staff as the "James Bond Room" the Touristorama (#33) has a mattress set in a round frame that turns with the flick of a switch. Its bath is also very dramatic, closed off by plate glass and visible from the bedroom, while the shower is set in a rock and cascading waterfall. Family units housed in a nondescript building—less desirable in terms of setting and decor but very practical—are the only four without a view. Standard rooms are a bit smaller with no terrace. The reception is in the main building, and the stubli/bar makes a cozy spot to settle in front of the fire. The more formal restaurant has windows looking out to the terrace where tables are set in warmer weather. Your sense of adventure in dining can be indulged in the Adventure Restaurant, a cave-like room set under a ceiling of stars and moons. *Directions:* Arriving in Brienz, drive up the hill 100 meters after the station.

HOSTELLERIE LINDENHOF
Owner: Fotsch-Wermuth
Lindenhofweg, Haus im Grünen
CH-3855 Brienz, Switzerland
Tel: (033) 952 20 30, Fax: (033) 952 20 40
40 rooms, Double: CHF 160–CHF 260
Open: mid-Mar to Dec, Credit cards: all major
18 km W of Interlaken, Train: 100 meters
Region: Bern
karenbrown.com/switzerland/lindenhof.html

You can just catch a glimpse of the orange wash and single gray-slated turret of the Grandhotel Giessbach peeking out from the dense forest across the lake from the town of Brienz. The only approach to Giessbach is by a single, narrow road accessed from the east side of the lake that often accommodates only one car and is closed in winter. Tucked just in a bend of the Giessbach Falls, this is a wonderful old grande dame of a hotel—quite regal, set on a ledge overlooking the lake. Even if you come only for tea and cake, the journey will be well rewarded. Tables set on the terrace enjoy unobstructed views of the turquoise-green waters of Brienz, and the constant drone of the waterfall mutes conversation. Quite lovely, the restaurant is found on the first floor, its expanse of windows overlooking the waterfall. The reception is found on the second floor and is accompanied by large, grand salons. There are four suites in each of the three turrets— the Clara Von Rappard Suite enjoys views of both lake and waterfall. The Bellevue Rooms, of which there are 13, are the best value and have wonderful views—my favorite is room 219 with a superb view of the lake and its own private small balcony. Standard rooms overlook the forest. The staff is quite professional and extremely gracious, and arrangements can be made for pickup at the airport or train station. *Directions:* Traveling the N8 between Interlaken and Brienz, exit at Brienz-Giessbach.

GRANDHOTEL GIESSBACH
Director: Matthias Kögl
Am Brienzersee
CH-3855 Brienz-Giessbach, Switzerland
Tel: (033) 952 25 25, Fax: (033) 952 25 30
70 rooms, Double: CHF 220–CHF 480
Open: Apr 18 to Oct 19, Credit cards: all major
18 km E of Interlaken on Lake Brienz, Train: 5 km
Region: Bern
karenbrown.com/switzerland/grandhotelgiessbach.html

When we first visited the Elvezia al Lago over 15 years ago, it was a sweet, modest little hotel. In spite of its simplicity we were captivated by its fabulous waterfront location and its blissful seclusion—it can be reached only by boat or by walking along a footpath along the edge of the lake. Today the romantic setting and seclusion remain unchanged, but the hotel's facilities have vastly improved over the years and there are now eight nicely furnished guestrooms, all with hairdryers, direct-dial phones, good bathrooms, televisions, and mini bars. Best of all, all but one of the bedrooms have a view. My personal favorites are the three rooms on the top floor, especially number 5, which is on the corner with windows on two sides to capture the vista. Another bonus is Elvezia al Lago's restaurant. Although there is a cozy dining room inside, usually guests eat out on a terrace that extends over the water. There is a boat dock in front where the ferry regularly pulls up with restaurant guests and there is also a waterfront garden with lounge chairs where guests can relax and enjoy a dip in the lake. *Directions:* You can take a ferry from Lugano to Grotto Elvezia, or drive along the lake from Lugano toward Castagnola and leave your car in the parking area where the small road Via Cortivo ends. Then either walk to the hotel (about eight minutes) or call the hotel for a boat to pick you up.

ELVEZIA AL LAGO   **New**
Owners: Doris & Herbert Lucke
Sentiero di Gandria 21
6976 Castagnola–Lugano, Switzerland
Tel: (091) 971 44 51, Fax: (091) 972 78 40
8 rooms, Double: CHF 180–CHF 230
Open: Apr to Nov, Credit cards: all major
3 km E of Lugano, Train: 3 km
Region: Ticino
karenbrown.com/switzerland/elvezialago.html

The Hostellerie Bon Accueil is an outstanding little inn, brimming with old-world charm. The weathered wood chalet accented by green shutters and windowboxes overflowing with geraniums dates back almost 300 years and still reflects the warmth and character of its farmhouse origins. Conveniently close to the famous ski resort of Gstaad, the inn hugs a sunny hillside overlooking Château d'Oex, a village famous for the production of cheese. Many chalet-style hotels look extremely appealing from the outside but most, disappointingly, seem to revert to a more sterile, modern ambiance once you enter the front door. Such is definitely not the case at the Hostellerie Bon Accueil. The owners have lovingly maintained a romantic, cozy appeal inside as well as out. The beautifully maintained hotel is endearing throughout, with low, beamed ceilings, soft lights, mellow wood paneling, and an abundance of country-style antiques. The guestrooms are as sweet as they can be, with pretty floral fabrics and cute white embroidered curtains accenting the windows. The food is excellent and the restaurant is lovely with candlelit dining. In summer, however, the large terrace is the favorite spot to enjoy a meal with a view of the mountains to whet the appetite. *Directions:* From Château d'Oex, cross the railroad tracks and follow signs up the hill to the hotel.

HOSTELLERIE BON ACCUEIL
Manager: Marianne Bon
CH-1660 Château d'Oex, Switzerland
Tel: (026) 924 63 20, Fax: (026) 924 51 26
18 rooms, Double: CHF 175–CHF 225
Closed: mid-Oct to mid-Dec, Credit cards: all major
15 km W of Gstaad, Train: 2 km
Region: Bern
karenbrown.com/switzerland/hostelleriebonaccueil.html

Chur, one of the oldest cities in Switzerland, retains a large, attractive medieval section with hidden squares, colorful fountains, remains of ancient walls, and an enticing network of cobbled streets. The Romantik Hotel Stern is situated in the heart of the charming old part of the city. Pink with green-shuttered windows, the building sits right on the street, but has a small garden terrace to the side. Inside, the public areas have many antique accents, but the bedrooms are standard in their furnishings, with light-knotty-pine furniture typical of the Grisons region. The building is 300 years old and has many nooks and crannies reached through a maze of hallways. This well-managed hotel's most attractive room is the charming restaurant with age-mellowed pine paneling and rustic-style chairs with carved hearts. Because Chur is on the main rail line, it makes a convenient hub for exploring Switzerland. Although most people think of Saint Moritz as the terminal for the Glacier Express (for more information see the itinerary section of this book), Chur is an alternative choice. *Directions:* Leave the autobahn from Zürich at Chur Nord, and go straight ahead for about 2 km. When the main road makes a right turn go straight into Reichgasse. There is free parking in the courtyard.

ROMANTIK HOTEL STERN
Owner: Brunner family
Reichgasse 11
CH-7000 Chur, Switzerland
Tel: (081) 258 57 57, Fax: (081) 258 57 58
66 rooms, Double: CHF 124–CHF 189
Open: all year, Credit cards: all major
120 km SE of Zürich, Train: 500 meters, free pickup
Region: Graubünden
karenbrown.com/switzerland/romantikhotelstern.html

The Hotel du Lac is located on Lake Geneva only about 12 kilometers east of Geneva. Although the hotel is on a busy road, behind the hotel is a pretty garden with a lawn stretching down to a private pier on the lake. The Hotel du Lac carries the air of an elegant home rather than that of a hotel. It does not appear very old, but it is: in fact, in 1626 the hotel was granted the exclusive right to receive and lodge people arriving by coach or horseback. At that time travelers on foot were excluded as guests of the inn because, as a memorandum dated 1768 decreed, "The titled man of wealth riding in his own coach and four must not be housed with the peasant, the knife-sharpener, the chimney-sweep—the latter would feel too ill at ease." The Hotel du Lac has been carefully restored and now you, too, can dream you are one of the guests arriving by "coach and four." The hotel has retained many of its old beams, stone walls, and lovely antique furniture and artifacts. All the bedrooms are attractive: some have kitchenettes, five suites have balconies with lake views, and some have a small terrace squeezed into the jumble of tiled rooftops. For those who want to be away from the city, the Hotel du Lac offers an appealing choice for visitors to Geneva. *Directions:* Between Geneva and Lausanne, by the Route du Lac. The hotel is located on the main street, by the lake.

HOTEL DU LAC
Owner: Oswald Schnyder
CH-1296 Coppet, Switzerland
Tel: (022) 77 61 521, Fax: (022) 77 65 346
18 rooms, Double: CHF 240–CHF 555*
*Breakfast not included: CHF 24
Open: all year, Credit cards: all major
12 km E of Geneva, Train: 1 km, Boat: 2 blocks
Region: Vaud
karenbrown.com/switzerland/relaishoteldulac.html

Le Vieux Chalet has a spectacular location high in the Jaunbach Pass, looking out across Lake Montsalvens over green pastures and forests to the distant castle of Gruyères and beyond to the towering, rugged mountains dominated by the dramatic peak of Moleson. The traditional chalet-style inn exudes an old-world charm with dark timbers, white stucco, deep overhanging eaves, and balconies heavily laden with flowers. The inside is just as appealing as the outside, with a most attractive, informal, pine-paneled dining room and a cozy, typically Alpine café where hikers often gather for lunch in summer. If the weather is fine, everyone drinks and eats on the spacious terrace where you can enjoy a panoramic Alpine view and excellent food. The five snug little bedrooms (three doubles, two singles) are pine-paneled and each has a small shower room. All have views but I especially like rooms 4, 5, and 6, which afford spectacular nighttime views of distant Gruyères when the castle is illuminated. Le Vieux Chalet has two large function rooms below it that are often used for summertime weddings. Crésuz-en-Gruyère is a convenient base for day trips to the charming hilltown of Gruyères or the beautiful city of Fribourg to the north. *Directions:* Leave the autobahn at Bulle and follow the signs for Gruyères. Take a left at the signpost for Charmey and follow this road for 6 km to Crésuz-en-Gruyère where you find Le Vieux Chalet to your left high above the road.

LE VIEUX CHALET
Owners: Jean-Claude & Jean-Pierre Sudan
CH-1653 Crésuz-en-Gruyère, Switzerland
Tel: (026) 927 12 86, Fax: (026) 927 22 86
5 rooms, Double: CHF 165–CHF
Closed: Jan to Feb 10, Credit cards: all major
29 km S of Fribourg, 20 min by bus from Bulle
Region: Fribourg
karenbrown.com/switzerland/levieux.html

The Auberge du Raisin is located in Cully, a sleepy, quaint, wine-growing village hugging the shore of Lake Geneva. A few minutes' walk from the hotel leads you down the hill to a lovely, tree-shaded park stretching along the waterfront—a perfect place to stroll while waiting for one of the lake steamers that pull into the dock. The fame of the Auberge du Raisin is based on its reputation for serving exceptional food accompanied by an extensive wine list featuring the finest wines from around the world. The chef, Adolfo Blokbergen, creates exceptional gourmet cuisine, attracting visitors from far and wide to his enchanting restaurant. The dining rooms, decorated with antique furnishings and highlighted by handsome old master paintings, exude a gentle, refined elegance that sets a romantic scene for the fine meals. The bedrooms too are outstanding. Individual in their decor, size, and arrangement, each is beautifully furnished in color-coordinated fabrics and maintained to perfection. Antiques are lavished throughout and are complemented by lovely, bountiful flower arrangements. This elegant, small Swiss inn, dating back to the 16th century, is a delightful place to stay while you explore one of Switzerland's most charming wine regions. *Directions:* Cully is a small town right on Lake Geneva, just 10 km southeast of Lausanne.

AUBERGE DU RAISIN
Managers: Mr & Mrs A. Blokbergen
1, Place de l'Hotel-de-Ville
CH-1096 Cully, Switzerland
Tel: (021) 799 21 31, Fax: (021) 799 25 01
10 rooms, Double: CHF 350–CHF 590
Open: all year, Credit cards: all major
70 km E of Geneva, Train: walking distance
Relais & Châteaux
Region: Vaud
karenbrown.com/switzerland/raisin.html

At the heart of one of Switzerland's finest wine-producing regions, Cully is wrapped by terraced fields of grapes on three sides and fronted by Lake Geneva. Cully is one of the most picturesque of the charming villages that dot the shores of the lake. Many ferryboats stop at Cully's small pier across from a grassy park. Facing the park and the lake is the superbly positioned Hotel Major Davel, a pink-stucco building with gray-green shutters and a mansard roof. Many diners come by boat and stop in Cully to enjoy lunch in the hotel's glass-enclosed terrace restaurant with a view of the lake. Rolf Messmer, the hotelier, is also the chef and the food is excellent. Those looking for a reasonably priced place to spend the night will find that the Hotel Major Davel offers, in addition to the restaurant, good accommodation. Upstairs (there is no elevator), the guestrooms are not deluxe, but certainly adequate. Rooms 5 and 10 are corner rooms with the advantage of having windows on two sides. With just 13 rooms, the owners pride themselves on the personalized service that they are able to offer their guests — and guests show their appreciation by repeated visits. Rolf and Bernadette are a young couple who bring a new enthusiasm and warmth to this wonderful country hotel. *Directions:* Cully is a small town on the shore of Lake Geneva, just 10 km southeast of Lausanne. The hotel is right on the waterfront.

HOTEL MAJOR DAVEL
Owners: Bernadette & Rolf Messmer
CH-1096 Cully, Switzerland
Tel: (021) 799 94 94, Fax: (021) 799 37 82
13 rooms, Double: CHF 180
Open: Jan 23 to Dec 10, Credit cards: MC, VS
70 km E of Geneva, Steps from boat dock
Region: Vaud
karenbrown.com/switzerland/hotelmajordavel.html

Dielsdorf is a small town north of Zürich, only about 20 minutes by car from the Zürich airport, or about 25 minutes from Zürich by train. The hotel is owned by Christa and Eugene Schäfer who also own the Rote Rose, a wonderful little inn only a few minutes away by car in the town of Regensberg. The Rote Rose is small, with only nine rooms, so it's nice to have this as a second choice. The Hotel Löwen, built in the 13th century, has been completely renovated. The outside is painted white with small gables and shuttered windows enhancing the country appeal. Floral paintings by Lotte Günthardt, Christa's mother, the world-renowned rose artist, adorn the walls throughout this small inn. The bedrooms are pleasantly decorated and the suite is an especially large, light, and airy room. If you are on a budget, a guestroom without a private bath is a good value. The most attractive feature of the hotel is the very cozy dining room where beamed ceilings, pretty linens, antique accents, and fresh-flower arrangements combine to create an inviting mood—and the food is excellent. *Directions:* Just to the north of Zürich, take the Zürich/Affoltern/Regensdorf exit from the A1 then take the main road to Dielsdorf/Koblenz. The hotel is in the center of the village.

HOTEL LÖWEN
Owners: Christa & Eugene Schäfer
Managers: Elizabeth & Louis Bourdon
Hinterdorfstrasse 21, CH-8157 Dielsdorf, Switzerland
Tel: (01) 855 61 61, Fax: (01) 855 61 62
35 rooms, Double: CHF 120–CHF 250*
*Breakfast not included: CHF 10
Closed: Jul 26 to Aug 9, Credit cards: all major
20 km N of Zürich airport, Train: 300 meters
Region: Zürich
karenbrown.com/switzerland/lowen.html

To reach Engelberg you leave the shores of Lake Lucerne and weave through a gorgeous narrow mountain valley. There is just one road in and at the end of the valley the road climbs a switchback passage to Engelberg, a town set in the shadow of towering peaks. It is a skiers' haven in the winter and in summer the high mountain valleys offer inviting opportunities for walking, hiking, and parasailing. Unable to find a hotel with old-world charm, we found a hotel with the most convenient location, the best views, and good value. Sitting on a lawn just a garden's distance from the tram station for Titlis, the four-story Hotel Sonnwendhof is newly built of white stucco, trimmed in wood, and colored with geranium-filled flowerboxes. There is no other building between it and the base of the mountain to obstruct Alpine views. Guestrooms are light and airy in their decor, with light pines used for the ceilings, window and door frames, and the furnishings. Beds are topped with plump down comforters and every room enjoys a comfortable sitting area. Rooms looking up to Titlis are premium, especially top-floor rooms set under vaulted ceilings. Guestrooms on the other side look up to the peaks of Brunni. Public areas include a small bar, an attractive, simply decorated restaurant, and a central garden courtyard terrace. *Directions:* Take the autobahn south from Lucerne and exit at Stans. From Stans travel 20 km on the 130 to Engelberg.

HOTEL SONNWENDHOF
Owner: Martin Faes
Gerschniweg 1
CH-6390 Engelberg, Switzerland
Tel: (041) 637 45 75, Fax: (041) 637 42 38
28 rooms, Double: CHF 160–CHF 240
Open: all year, Credit cards: all major
32 km SE of Lucerne, Train: 5 km
Region: Obwalden
karenbrown.com/switzerland/sonnwendhof.html

Geneva is known for its lovely lakeside hotels, but an appealing hotel exists in that quaint old section of the city—the Hotel les Armures, converted from a private residence dating from the 17th century. The mood and ambiance is intimate. There are no signs of tour groups, only guests sitting in a small lounge, talking quietly or reading—using the hotel as they would their homes. All the guestrooms have handsome wood doors and are decorated with traditional pieces and antiques. The standard room I occupied on my visit had a queen-sized bed, a small round table, antique-style high-backed armchairs, bedside tables with lamps, a small refrigerator, and a very nice bathroom with a hairdryer. The room was quite small but cozy, with a beamed ceiling and wood-framed windows looking over a quiet, shaded square and old fountain. Junior suites offer more spacious accommodation than the standard rooms. Personal favorites in the category of standard room are 201 with its beautiful 17th-century hand-painted beams and courtyard overlook and 401 with its lovely antique furnishings. Set against the exposed stone walls, rooms 407 and 409 are especially lovely junior suites. When making a reservation, request detailed directions as the hotel is a bit difficult to find and request a room overlooking the square. The hotel has a restaurant, staggered over three levels. *Directions:* Located in the old town at the foot of Saint Peter's Cathedral.

HOTEL LES ARMURES
Owner: Nicole Borgeat
1, Rue du Puits St. Pierre
CH-1204 Geneva, Switzerland
Tel: (022) 310 91 72, Fax: (022) 310 98 46
28 rooms, Double: CHF 500–CHF 635
Open: all year, Credit cards: all major
At the heart of old town, Train: 2 km
Region: Geneva
karenbrown.com/switzerland/amures.html

Well located just off the Quai General Guisan, a block or so from the heart of the old pedestrian quarter of Geneva as well as convenient to the lake, the Hotel de la Cigogne offers the ultimate in personalized service and luxurious accommodation. The atmosphere reminds me of an exclusive club. It is gorgeous. Furnishings throughout the hotel are elegant and ornate. The sitting room off the lobby has painted murals and the intimate and beautifully paneled restaurant has a stained-glass ceiling. Guestrooms are individual in their decor, from the one modern room whose walls have been created to resemble a grotto, to the other 51 rooms, all beautifully appointed and decorated with fine antiques from an assortment of periods and styles. Even the so-called standard rooms are comfortable in size, but the junior suites afford the spaciousness of an additional sitting area. The majority of the master suites are on two levels and enjoy the added luxury of two bathrooms, one off the bedroom and one off the living room or salon. All guestrooms have private bathrooms, all with bathtubs—there are no showers at this hotel. Air conditioning is by ice-cool circulating water, which gives many health and comfort benefits. *Directions:* From the airport keep to Centre Ville after the Mont Blanc Bridge. Drive approximately 150 meters and do not turn left or right. The hotel is easy to spot with its orange awnings and ornamental gold stork, La Cigogne.

HOTEL DE LA CIGOGNE
Owner: René Favre
17, Place Longemalle
CH-1204 Geneva, Switzerland
Tel: (022) 818 40 40, Fax: (022) 818 40 50
52 rooms, Double: CHF 455–CHF 890
Open: all year, Credit cards: all major
At the heart of old town, Train: 1 km
Relais & Châteaux
Region: Geneva
karenbrown.com/switzerland/cigogne.html

This lovely hotel, while three-star in rating, shares the same four-star attitude in terms of service as its regal neighbor, Hotel de la Cigogne. The location on the tranquil Place Longemalle is peaceful and the entry is dramatic with a hand-painted imported bar serving as the reception. The decor of the hotel is influenced by the owner's appreciation and use of color. Just steps up from the lobby is an inviting bar with the cozy ambiance of a British pub. Fifty-eight guestrooms are distributed over six floors, each floor sporting a different color theme. I was able to see a full range of rooms: 609 is a lovely corner room under angled ceilings that profits from windows on two sides that overlook the myriad of rooftops; 602 is a superior suite, cozy under heavy beams, and enjoys a lovely sitting area; and the manager's favorite, 607, staggered over three floors, enjoys a separate sitting area, a bedroom, a loft, and a spectacular private rooftop terrace boasting the best views in Geneva. Breakfast is a lavish buffet offered in a gorgeous room with pine floors and views out through an expanse of floor-to-ceiling arched windows. Running the length of the room is an outdoor terrace where chairs are nestled up against a wrought-iron railing and windowboxes overflow with red geraniums. *Directions:* Just after crossing the Mont Blanc Bridge, follow directions to Centre Ville and you come to Place Longemalle.

HOTEL TOURING-BALANCE
Owner: René Favre
Manager: Philippe Vuillemin
13, Place Longemalle
CH-1204 Geneva, Switzerland
Tel: (022) 818 62 62, Fax: (022) 818 62 61
58 rooms, Double: CHF 275–CHF 500
Open: all year, Credit cards: all major
At the heart of the old town, Train: 2 km
Region: Geneva
karenbrown.com/switzerland/touring.html

The medieval village of Hermance, located 15 minutes from Geneva's city center on the south shore of Lake Geneva, is the last community you come to before entering France. Easily accessible from Geneva by bus, car, or boat, the Auberge d'Hermance offers a nice alternative to city hotels. Located on a quiet side street about a block from the lake, the auberge is best known as an excellent countryside restaurant and guests come from far and near to dine. The centuries-old house has a terrace in front where tables are beautifully set in the "wintergarden" heated in winter for cozy, sunlit dining on chilly days. When it gets really cold, the indoor dining area enjoys a warm hearth. The specialty of the restaurant is poulet ou loup de mer cuit en croûte de sel, which comprises either a chicken or a sea bass baked in a shell of large-grain salt so thick that it looks like a rock, which the waiter dramatically breaks open at the table with a wooden hammer. Most dinner guests never realize that upstairs from the restaurant there are six guestrooms available. The two that are least expensive are very good value, but also very small. If you want more luxury, splurge on one of the suites. *Directions:* Enter the city of Geneva and follow the sign to Le Lac, Evian. Drive along the lake for approximately 6 km until you reach Vesenaz. At the first crossroads, turn left in the direction of Hermance. Drive for 8 km in the countryside into Hermance.

AUBERGE D'HERMANCE
Owner: Franz Wehren
Manager: Antonio Manteigas
12, Rue du Midi
CH-1248 Geneva–Hermance, Switzerland
Tel: (022) 75 11 368, Fax: (022) 75 11 631
6 rooms, Double: CHF 240–CHF 450
Closed: Feb 15 to Mar 3, Credit cards: all major
16 km E of Geneva, Bus: 20 min to Geneva
Region: Geneva
karenbrown.com/switzerland/aubergedhermance.html

Perched high in the hills above Montreux, the Hotel Victoria (a member of the Relais & Châteaux group) is a handsome hotel with a mansard roof. From the hotel, the pool, and the perfectly manicured gardens terraced below, there is a truly breathtaking panorama of Lake Geneva backed by jagged mountain peaks. From the moment you walk inside this beautiful inn, there is an old-world ambiance enhanced by handsome antique furniture. There are many niches in the various lounges where guests can relax—one of my favorites is the cheerful, bright, garden "sun room"—a delightful spot to enjoy a good book or afternoon tea. The bar area is inviting, with dark paneling enhanced by old paintings. There are two elegantly decorated dining rooms serving superb meals. The owner, Mr Mittermair, mingles throughout the dining room at dinner to make sure that his guests are well cared for. The guestrooms have been completely renovated and glamorous new suites added, with views so spectacular that you will never want to leave your room. Although this is a grand hotel, it is run with such warmth and fine management, you will feel like a guest in a private home. Compared to what you would pay to stay at a hotel in Geneva, the Victoria is a great value. *Directions:* Located 90 km from Geneva Cointrin airport, on the Montreux Rochers de Naye railway line, 10 minutes from the Montreux or Villeneuve motorway exits.

HOTEL VICTORIA
Owner: Toni Mittermair
CH-1823 Glion–Montreux, Switzerland
Tel: (021) 962 82 82, Fax: (021) 962 82 92
60 rooms, Double: CHF 250–CHF 580
Open: all year, Credit cards: all major
90 km E of Geneva, Train: 200 meters, free pickup
Relais & Châteaux
Region: Vaud
karenbrown.com/switzerland/hotelvictoriasw.html

The setting of the Hotel Krone is idyllic. Just across the street from the hotel, the River Rhine flows by and narrows on its course from Lake Constance. The Krone has an outdoor terrace on the banks of the river, with a cluster of small tables where meals are served in warm weather. When I first stayed at the Hotel Krone, I fell in love with this beautiful small inn, so well managed by the gracious Schraner-Michaeli family, who personally pamper each guest. The guestrooms have all been totally redone, each individual in decor and each lovely. My favorites were those decorated in a French style with beautiful rose-patterned fabrics. There are only two rooms that actually overlook the water, rooms 220 and 222. The intimate dining room remains, as always, an elegant, paneled room with tables exquisitely set with crisp linens and fresh flowers. Best yet, the food is exceptional. The Hotel Krone makes an excellent base for exploring the northern region of Switzerland and just steps from the door you can board the ferry that will take you along the Rhine. On a day's boat excursion you can visit the delightful village of Stein am Rhein with its wonderfully painted buildings or the medieval town of Schaffhausen. *Directions:* Gottlieben is located on the Untersee approximately 5 km to the west of Konstanz and the Bodensee. It is a small town and the Krone is right on the waterfront.

ROMANTIK HOTEL KRONE
Owner: Georg Schraner
Seestrasse 11
CH-8274 Gottlieben, Switzerland
Tel: (071) 666 80 60, Fax: (071) 666 80 69
25 rooms, Double: CHF 180–CHF 300
Closed: mid-Jan to mid-Feb, Credit cards: all major
5 km W of Constance, Rhine ferry across from hotel
Region: Thurgau
karenbrown.com/switzerland/romantikhotelkrone.html

It was love at first sight when I came to Grimentz, a tumble of storybook, dark-timbered chalets accented with colorful flowers, sitting high in the Anniviers Valley. How fortunate that at the entrance to the old village is the delightful, family-run Hotel de Moiry, a whitewashed inn with handsome wood shutters. Even if you are unable to spend several nights here, this is an excellent place to enjoy, as we did on our first visit to Grimentz, a hearty lunch of fondue, salad, and crusty dark bread, leaving just enough room for a slice of strudel. On warm days you eat outside on the terrace or, if the weather is inclement, in the cozy, traditional dining room before a blazing fire kept lit to make raclette. How fortunate that we were able to return to spend the night and enjoy a traditional raclette dinner of grilled cheese, potatoes, gherkins, and little onions, in the convivial company of a group of hikers spending a week walking in the mountains. There is nothing fancy about the hotel—it is genuine, old-time Swiss. Upstairs, the simple bedrooms have crisp-white walls and pine paneling and each is accompanied by a shower room. *Directions:* From Lausanne take the A9 autobahn to Sierre where you follow signs for Val d'Anniviers, which winds you up the mountains for the 30-km drive to Grimentz.

HOTEL DE MOIRY
Owners: Andrea & Aurel Salamin-Walker
CH-3961 Grimentz, Switzerland
Tel: (027) 475 11 44, Fax: (027) 475 28 23
17 rooms, Double: CHF 110–CHF 160
Open: Dec 18 to May & Jun to Nov, Credit cards: MC, VS
55 km SW of Brig, Train to Sierre, 1 hr by postal bus
Region: Valais
karenbrown.com/switzerland/hoteldemoiry.html

The Gletschergarten, built in 1899, sits in a meadow of wildflowers, overlooking a glacier. Originally a large family home, the house gradually evolved into a small hotel. While helping her parents, Elsbeth met Finn Breitenstein, a member of the Danish ski team housed at the Gletschergarten. On the last day of the competition, Finn had an accident that delayed his departure—the rest is history. Elsbeth and Finn fell in love and today they are the third generation to operate the Chalet Gletschergarten, continuing the tradition of outstanding hospitality. (The Breitenstein family celebrated their 100th anniversary of innkeeping in 1999.) The hotel is filled with old-world charm, with pine-paneled walls, antique accents, original oil paintings by Elsbeth's father, and Oriental carpets. The cozily paneled dining room serves excellent food (be sure to take demi-pension). The bedrooms are attractive, all opening onto flower-laden balconies that wrap completely around each floor of the hotel. The rooms in front overlook the mountains, but I fell in love with our accommodation (room 21), a quiet room in the back with a pretty view of green hills. There is a motto on the front of this delightful inn that truly reflects its spirit and hospitality: "Gladness to the ones that arrive. Freedom to the ones that stay here. Blessing to the ones that move on." *Directions:* One km up the main street from the station immediately after the town church.

CHALET-HOTEL GLETSCHERGARTEN
Owners: Elsbeth & Finn Breitenstein
CH-3818 Grindelwald, Switzerland
Tel: (033) 853 17 21, Fax: (033) 853 29 57
26 rooms, Double: CHF 210–CHF 280
Open: Dec to Mar & Jun to Oct, Credit cards: all major
20 km SE of Interlaken, Train: 1 km
Region: Bern
karenbrown.com/switzerland/gletschergarten.html

The small, shuttered, chalet-style Hotel Fiescherblick sits on the main street, overlooking Grindelwald's picturesque little church. The hotel is not fancy, but does possess a most inviting atmosphere. As you enter the lobby, the mood is set by a great old Swiss clock, a painted Swiss wall cupboard, a little table paired with a regional Alpine chair, and a few very old milking stools. I was intrigued with the many little niches throughout the hotel artistically displaying antique farm implements. Mr Brawand explained that the inn was originally his family's home and the various farm tools were used on his father's farm. In one area you find a number of cheese-making utensils, churns, a milking stool, sieves, and wooden frames. Olivier Bricka is the chef and has earned the restaurant many accolades. The hotel has two dining rooms—one is quite elegant, and the other, a bistro, offers regional specialties in a rustic setting. When the weather is warm, meals are also served outside on a street-level terrace. All of the guestrooms are fresh and charming and all enjoy small balconies. The guests on shorter stays often request the rooms at the front overlooking the town and spectacular mountain views, while longer-stay guests prefer the quiet of the back rooms overlooking fields grazed by cattle. *Directions:* The Fiescherblick is located on the main street of town, opposite the church.

HOTEL FIESCHERBLICK
Owner: Johannes Brawand
CH-3818 Grindelwald, Switzerland
Tel: (033) 854 53 53, Fax: (033) 854 53 50
25 rooms, Double: CHF 200–CHF 280
Open: Jun to Oct & Dec to Easter, Credit cards: all major
20 km SE of Interlaken, Train: 1 km
Region: Bern
karenbrown.com/switzerland/hotelfiescherblick.html

The Hostellerie de Saint Georges is a delightful hotel, enthusiastically run by Eugènia and Christian Frossard, in the heart of the beautiful hilltop, walled, medieval village of Gruyères. The hotel is named for old Saint George himself—you will see our mighty hero slaying the dragon on the brightly colored emblem proudly displayed over the front door, and again on a carving hung over an antique chest in the main hallway. Each bedroom door displays a motif from the era of Saint George. On the door of one room there is a whimsical knight with sword raised high, on another a musician playing an instrument similar to a bagpipe, while yet another has a witch-like character riding a broom. The most expensive rooms (2 and 3) are spacious and lovely, with stunning views across the ramparts to the mountains. By comparison, the rest of the rooms are snug and simply decorated. If you are not able to reserve a room with a view, do not worry for you can enjoy the same view from the enclosed terrace where lunch and dinner are served. The menu naturally features local specialties made from Gruyères cheese. The quiche is so incomparably light, with such a delicate pastry, that it is tempting to order it at every meal. Another dining room specializes in food cooked to order on the open grill. *Directions:* Leave the autobahn at Bulle and follow the signs for Gruyères through Bulle. Drive into the village to unload and you will be directed to parking.

HOSTELLERIE DE SAINT GEORGES
Owner: Christian Frossard
CH-1663 Gruyères, Switzerland
Tel: (026) 921 83 00, Fax: (026) 921 83 39
14 rooms, Double: CHF 185–CHF 290
Closed: Nov, Dec & Jan, Credit cards: all major
35 km S of Fribourg, Train: 1 km
Region: Fribourg
karenbrown.com/switzerland/saintgeorges.html

The Hostellerie des Chevaliers, a member of the Relais du Silence group, is located just outside the walls of the medieval village of Gruyères, just beyond the parking area number 1. The hotel has been owned by the Corboz family for more than 25 years. The hotel is found in two buildings: the main one houses the bedrooms and the breakfast room and is connected by a tunnel to the adjacent chalet containing the restaurant. Guestrooms are found on each of three floors. All but room 24 (the largest room with drapes and walls in a floral decor) are simply decorated and each has a small bathroom. Rooms under the eaves are more spacious, often able to accommodate up to four persons. If possible, request one of the rooms with a balcony overlooking the valley. These back rooms have wonderful, unobstructed views of the walled village of Gruyères and across the rolling hills grazed by sheep and cows to high mountains. *Directions:* Leave the autobahn at Bulle and follow the signs for Gruyères through Bulle. Try to park in car park 1 but if you cannot, park in 2 or 3 and walk up to the hotel where you can often receive permission to park beside the hotel in its car park.

HOSTELLERIE DES CHEVALIERS
Owner: Corboz family
CH-1663 Gruyères, Switzerland
Tel: (026) 921 19 33, Fax: (026) 921 33 13
34 rooms, Double: CHF 190–CHF 250
Closed: Jan, Credit cards: all major
35 km S of Fribourg, Train: 1 km (in Gruyères/Pringy)
Region: Fribourg
karenbrown.com/switzerland/deschevaliers.html

Travelers idealize Switzerland and hope to discover their dream—a storybook land of sweet chalets, windowboxes adorned with geraniums, balconies overlooking lush meadows, the gentle melody of cow bells, cozy furnishings, adorable villages, soaring mountains, and great food. All expectations are fulfilled at Le Grand Chalet. The hotel, built in the 1990s, mimics the chalet style seen in the quaint old farmhouses that dot the landscape. A small road winds up the hill from Gstaad (an exceptionally picturesque small village) to the beautifully positioned Grand Chalet. There is a light and airy look, fresh and pretty, filled with charm. The walls are white, the beams and paneling of blond wood, the Alpine-style furniture upholstered with pretty, country fabric, and frilly white curtains peek from beneath blue draperies. The living room, bar, and dining room flow together into a spacious room highlighted by a superb, old-world fireplace that warms all the rooms. Large windows in the dining room look over a splendid vista of green valley and beyond to the soaring mountains. This same picture-perfect view is captured from the balconies of the deluxe guestrooms. The owners of this intimate hotel, Josette and Franz Rosskogler, are gracious, caring hosts who ensure every detail is perfect and welcome guests as friends. *Directions:* From the north, turn left before the pedestrian section of Gstaad, following signs to the hotel.

LE GRAND CHALET
Owners: Josette & Franz Rosskogler
CH-3780 Gstaad, Switzerland
Tel: (033) 748 76 76, Fax: (033) 748 76 77
20 rooms, Double: CHF 260–CHF 750
Open: Jun to mid-Oct & Dec to Apr, Credit cards: all major
88 km E of Geneva, Train: 1 km
Region: Bern
karenbrown.com/switzerland/legrandchalet.html

The Hotel Olden, a tradition for those in the know who visit Gstaad, is a chalet-style, cream-colored inn embellished with flowers, cheerful green shutters, and windowboxes of red geraniums. This charming inn is a favorite of everyone, including the rich and famous who come in winter to ski. After a day on the slopes, guests gather in the bar for après-ski relaxation. In summer, dining outside on the terrace is a popular alternative to the lovely candlelit dining room where the live background music gives a romantic, supper-club atmosphere. In winter, dinner in the intimate cellar restaurant is a must. Bedrooms are found in the main building—delightful, luxuriously appointed traditional rooms—and in the chalet connected to the hotel by a rooftop terrace. With their luxurious, traditional decor, these chalet rooms are a must if you are under 6 feet tall (the height of the ceilings). Guests come back year after year in appreciation of the inviting rooms and outstanding food. *Directions:* Arriving in Gstaad, follow signs for Ober-Gstaad then the signpost to the hotel. Parking is either behind the hotel or in its private garage.

HOTEL OLDEN
Manager: Urs Eberhardt
CH-3780 Gstaad, Switzerland
Tel: (033) 744 34 44, Fax: (033) 744 61 64
16 rooms, Double: CHF 300–CHF 1500
Closed: Apr & Oct, Credit cards: all major
88 km E of Geneva, Train: 3-minute walk
Region: Bern
karenbrown.com/switzerland/hotelolden.html

The Post Hotel Rössli has been in Ruedi Widmer's family since 1922. Ruedi was in his youth an ardent Alpine climber and skier. He still retains his qualifications but nowadays confines his guiding to taking guests on organized mountain walks, offering a program where he and several other guides lead excursions of climbing, walking, and generally enjoying the exquisite beauty of the area. It's refreshing to stay here at a traditional family hotel in a chic resort and experience old-style Swiss hospitality. The Alpine-style café bar is a gathering place for locals and guests alike—an excellent casual dining spot—though in summer it would be a shame not to eat outside in the garden opposite the hotel. As an alternative to the café there is a very nice restaurant specializing in traditional Swiss fare. Upstairs, you find reception, the bedrooms, and an eclectically decorated sitting room with old photos of the town on the walls alongside Ruedi's first hunting trophies. The pine-paneled bedrooms vary from light pine to mellow old pine— ask for a recently remodeled room (they have the nicest bathrooms). Standard rooms come with very snug shower rooms while the superior have more spacious bathrooms. *Directions:* Arriving in Gstaad, follows signs for the hotel, unload your luggage, and you will be directed to nearby parking.

POST HOTEL RÖSSLI
Owner: Ruedi Widmer
CH-3780 Gstaad, Switzerland
Tel: (033) 748 42 42, Fax: (033) 748 42 43
18 rooms, Double: CHF 190–CHF 310
Closed: May, Credit cards: all major
88 km E of Geneva, Train: 5-minute walk
Region: Bern
karenbrown.com/switzerland/posthotelrossli.html

Guarda, a cluster of old, intricately painted farmhouses with flowers at every window, nestles on a mountain shelf high above the Engadine Valley—one of the most picturesque hideaways in Switzerland. Happily, there is a gem of a hotel to match the perfection of the village. The Hotel Meisser is beautifully situated overlooking the expanse of green valley below, with a terrace where guests can enjoy refreshments served by waitresses in local costume. The hotel, a typical Engadine farmhouse, dates back to the 17th century. Throughout the hotel there is an old-world ambiance achieved through the use of antique chests, pieces of old copper, oil paintings, and baskets of fresh flowers everywhere. The main house offers simple accommodation, and two front corner rooms (15 and 16) afford memorable views and enjoy their own balconies. Across the street the converted farmhouse, Chasa Pepina, houses La Charpenna, a spectacular penthouse suite with pine beams and unobstructed hillside views, and the Stuva Veglia with its beautiful wood walls and floor—the accommodation is elegant and superbly appointed. The Meisser is truly a favorite for all its wealth of attributes and the wonderful family for which it is named. Settle in here for several days to appreciate one of Switzerland's most beautiful valleys and hotels. *Directions:* From the 27 between Susch and Scuol, exit at Giarsun on a small road that winds up to the village of Guarda.

HOTEL MEISSER
Owners: Kathrine & Ralf Benno & Beno Meisser
CH-7545 Guarda, Switzerland
Tel: (081) 862 21 32, Fax: (081) 862 24 80
30 rooms, Double: CHF 210–CHF 480
Open: all year, Credit cards: all major
81 km NE of St. Moritz, 2 ½ hrs from Zürich airport
Region: Graubünden
karenbrown.com/switzerland/hotelmeisser.html

Several readers have written to us recommending the Hotel Krebs as their favorite place to stay in Interlaken. This is not a tiny inn (it even caters to small groups), but somehow the owners, Marian and Peter Koschak, extend such a genuine warmth of welcome that guests feel very special. The hotel has been handed down through four generations of the Krebs family. On the first floor are several small lounges, comfortable and homey with an old-fashioned ambiance and decorated with cherished family pieces such as the handsome grandfather clock and old pewter coffeepots from the 1870s and the hotel's origin. To the right of the reception are three dining rooms opening onto each other. The bedrooms are all individually and simply decorated with a few well-chosen pieces. Prime are the front corner rooms and, of those, a favorite, room 104, has lovely old furnishings and a beautiful mirror. The back rooms are quieter, but those in front have a view of the Jungfrau. I was surprised that the mountains could be seen from its downtown location, but Mrs Koschak told me that her great-grandfather negotiated with the city fathers that no tall buildings could be built to obstruct the view. *Directions:* Bahnhofstrasse is the main road through town and Hotel Krebs fronts the street.

HOTEL KREBS
Owners: Marian & Peter Koschak-Krebs
Bahnhofstrasse 4
CH-3800 Interlaken, Switzerland
Tel: (033) 822 71 61, Fax: (033) 823 24 65
49 rooms, Double: CHF 230–CHF 300
Open: Apr 25 to Oct 25, Credit cards: all major
59 km SE of Bern, Train: 2-minute walk
Region: Bern
karenbrown.com/switzerland/hotelkrebs.html

The Hotel du Lac, owned by the Hofmann family for over 100 years, is more French than Swiss in appearance, with a gray mansard roof and pink façade. The hotel is located directly on the banks of the River Aare as it flows between the two lakes of Brienz and Thun. Bedrooms at the back overlook the river—a peaceful scene of boats and swans gliding below—while those at the front are less blessed, with street and rooftop views. There are two dining rooms and one, the Restaurant Rivière, is especially appealing, with large windows opening onto lovely river views. In recent years, all 40 guestrooms have been refurbished and all now offer modern comfort and a somewhat modern decor. Although the Hotel du Lac is large, the management does discourage conference and group bookings at the height of season, and if you want a convenient base for excursions, it cannot be surpassed. We include the Hotel du Lac especially for those readers traveling by public transportation as the location is so convenient—just steps from where the trains depart for the Jungfraujoch excursion and minutes from the dock where the boats leave for exploring Lake Brienz. *Directions:* From the motorway, exit Interlaken-Ost (East), turn right, and pass the train station. The hotel is behind the station.

HOTEL DU LAC
Owner: Hofmann family
Hoheweg 225
CH-3800 Interlaken, Switzerland
Tel: (033) 822 29 22, Fax: (033) 822 29 15
40 rooms, Double: CHF 220–CHF 310
Open: mid-Mar to mid-Nov, Credit cards: all major
59 km SE of Bern, Train & boat: 100 meters
Region: Bern
karenbrown.com/switzerland/hoteldulacsw.html

The Landgasthof Ruedihus is the perfect Swiss inn, exactly what I'd always hoped to discover, but had almost decided did not exist except in my dreams: a cozy, flower-laden chalet, nestled in a lush meadow, backed by mountains and brimming inside and out with antique charm. This tiny chalet, dating back to 1753, is fashioned entirely of wood, darkened through the years and decorated with both carved and painted peasant designs. Two rows of small bottle-glass windows stretch across the front of the house, highlighted by boxes of red geraniums. Inside, the romance continues—every room is a dream. Appropriate country antiques are used throughout. Most of the bedrooms have genuine antiques, and those that do not, have beautifully crafted reproductions. Some of the bedrooms have a view of the mountains, but because of the authentic nature of the building, some rooms have small windows peeking out from under the deep eaves. However, no matter which bedroom you choose, if you enjoy an old-world ambiance, you will be happy—each one is enchanting. Although there are only nine bedrooms, the inn has its own well-equipped kitchen, and excellent meals are served in the intimate dining room. Note: Reservations are handled by the Waldhotel Doldenhorn—see next listing. *Directions:* After passing the center of the village, you will find the inn on the right-hand side of the street.

LANDGASTHOF RUEDIHUS
Owner: René Maeder
CH-3718 Kandersteg, Switzerland
Tel: (033) 675 81 81, Fax: (033) 675 81 85
9 rooms, Double: CHF 210–CHF 260
Open: all year, Credit cards: all major
45 km SW of Interlaken, Train: 2 km
Region: Bern
karenbrown.com/switzerland/landgasthofruedihus.html

The Waldhotel Doldenhorn is beautifully positioned at the end of the Kandersteg Valley, with the wooded mountains rising precipitously behind the hotel. There are two sections to the hotel, the main building and an adjacent chalet (where the guestrooms are less expensive). Registration is in the main hotel. Steps lead up to a reception area opening onto an attractively decorated lounge with dark paneling, handsome striped fabric on high-backed chairs, and intimate groupings of leather chairs. Beyond the lounge is the Grüner Saal, an elegant, rather formal, dining room with green-striped draperies framing large windows, silver chandeliers, and tables properly set with pretty linens and fresh flowers. The Restaurant Burestube is a wood-paneled dining room with rustic wooden chairs and milk-glass lamps hanging from the decoratively paneled wood ceiling. Each of the bedrooms is individually decorated, many with lovely antiques. One of the more expensive but especially lovely rooms is 109, a spacious bedroom with beautiful antique furniture and a pretty view. Anne and René Maeder also own the Landgasthof Ruedihus across the road. The Ruedihus exudes a rustic ambiance, while the Doldenhorn displays a more formal charm. The hotel also has a wellness center with three saunas, whirlpool, and solarium. *Directions:* After passing the town center, you will find the hotel on the left-hand side of the street.

WALDHOTEL DOLDENHORN
Owner: René Maeder
CH-3718 Kandersteg, Switzerland
Tel: (033) 675 81 81, Fax: (033) 675 81 85
34 rooms, Double: CHF 270–CHF 600
Closed: Apr & Nov, Credit cards: all major
45 km SW of Interlaken, Train: 2 km
Region: Bern
karenbrown.com/switzerland/waldhoteldoldenhorn.html

I visited the Chesa Grischuna for inclusion in the first edition of our guide to Switzerland and 12 years later the vivid memories of that visit lingered with such pleasure that I knew if the hotel still existed, I would want to include it. The season was different, winter's cozy blanket of snow having given way with spring to clusters of brightly colored flowers, but the interior was as I remembered—romantic and warm. Mellow, weathered paneling enriches most of the public rooms, while antique furnishings and accents of copper pieces and artistic flower arrangements blend beautifully. Without the benefit of antiques, the bedrooms achieve the country feeling, utilizing charming provincial wallpapers and matching fabrics, copies of traditional Swiss furniture, exposed beams, and gently sloping floors. Some of the bedrooms are small, but all are nicely decorated. If you are on a budget, you might want to consider a room without bath. The dining room, with a country-formal atmosphere, is exceptional in cuisine and service. The personality of the staff matches the character and charm of the inn. The Romantik Hotel Chesa Grischuna never disappoints us—it always remains a favorite. *Directions:* From Landquart, exit the highway and take the road in the direction of Davos. Once in Klosters, after passing the old church, take the next right in the direction of the train station. The hotel is in the center of the village.

ROMANTIK HOTEL CHESA GRISCHUNA
Owner: Guler family
Bahnhofstrasse 12
CH-7250 Klosters, Switzerland
Tel: (081) 422 22 22, Fax: (081) 422 22 25
25 rooms, Double: CHF 180–CHF 440
Closed: mid-Oct to mid-Dec & mid-Apr to Jul
Credit cards: all major
40 km E of Chur, Train: 200 meters
Region: Graubünden
karenbrown.com/switzerland/grischuna.html

The Hotel du Lac Seehof is in Küssnacht, a small town on Lake Lucerne and a stop for many of the steamers that ply the lake. The hotel is ideally situated directly on the waterfront where the boats dock and serves as a popular luncheon spot. The town of Küssnacht is bustling with tourists, but there is a feeling of tranquillity in the oasis of the hotel's terrace restaurant, which is very popular with day-trippers from Lucerne. The hotel has been in the Trutmann family for five generations and is now managed by Albert Trutmann and his attractive wife, Joan. Albert Trutmann lived in the United States for a number of years, speaks perfect English, and understands American tastes. Joan hails from Tahiti and has added her exotic island touch with the Blue Lagoon conservatory on the waterfront. In inclement weather guests dine inside in a series of attractive dining rooms. The food is excellent, with fish being featured on the menu. Upstairs, all the bedrooms, found off broad corridors, have simple decor and spotless shower rooms. Several have a traditional piece of furniture. *Directions:* From Zürich exit the N4 at Küssnacht and follow signposts to the lakefront and ferry.

HOTEL DU LAC SEEHOF
Owners: Joan & Albert Trutmann-de Brath
Seeplatz 6
CH-6403 Küssnacht am Rigi, Switzerland
Tel: (041) 850 10 12, Fax: (041) 850 10 22
14 rooms, Double: CHF 190–CHF 220
Closed: Nov, Credit cards: all major
13 km NE of Lucerne, Train: 1 km
Region: Schwyz
karenbrown.com/switzerland/dulacseehof.html

As you drive through the village of Lenzerheide, you are surrounded by the commercialism of a major ski resort—too modern, too new. But follow the signs to Sporz, into the hills, and suddenly you are in a high mountain hamlet. The area consists of mountain meadows enhanced by a backdrop of mighty mountain peaks. Nothing mars the landscape dotted by only a few weathered farmhouses. This is the location of the Romantik Hotel Guarda Val. At first glance you would never guess that a deluxe hotel is nestled in this tiny village, but closer inspection reveals a gourmet restaurant in one building, a Swiss and Italian regional restaurant in another, and guestrooms cleverly incorporated into a selection of smaller farmhouses. In winter the fields are blanketed with snow—a mecca for the skier. In summer the meadows are sprinkled with wildflowers and laced with paths—a delight for the hiker. The guestrooms, which vary from quite small rooms to suites, are all decorated with a modern flavor. Prices seem a bit high for value, but this is the best choice for accommodation in the area. There are two choices for dining: one is an elegant, well-known French restaurant, the other a cozy, stubli-style restaurant specializing in regional dishes. *Directions:* Lenzerheide is 18 km south of Chur. The Romantik Hotel Guarda Val is located on the outskirts of town and is signed from the city center.

ROMANTIK HOTEL GUARDA VAL
Owner: Erich Kurzen family
Val Sporz
CH-7078 Lenzerheide–Sporz, Switzerland
Tel: (081) 385 85 85, Fax: (081) 385 85 95
34 rooms, Double: CHF 220–CHF 934
Open: Jun to Apr 15, Credit cards: all major
120 km SW of Zürich, Train 2 km
Region: Graubünden
karenbrown.com/switzerland/hotelguarda.html

The Hotel des Balances, located on the banks of the River Reuss, has undergone an extensive renovation, transforming this potentially good, but previously somewhat dreary, hotel into a real winner. The unusual exterior remains unchanged. The riverside view of the building is white, highlighted with windowboxes brimming with blue, yellow, and pink petunias. The side of the hotel that faces a small square is totally covered with intricate paintings of angels, columns, warriors, costumed peasants, and flowers. From the hotel entrance, steps lead up to the lobby, which opens into a cheerful lounge with a colorful cluster of chairs and sofas. To the right of the lobby is the breakfast room, very attractive with large oil paintings on the walls. French doors from the lounge lead to a balcony overlooking the river. As you enter the hotel, if instead of going up to the lobby, you take the steps to the lower level, you will find the restaurant Rotes Gatter, with a delightful terrace looking out over the river, serving fine Swiss cuisine. The guestrooms are attractively decorated in pastel hues. The choice rooms, of course, are those with a balcony overlooking the river. *Directions:* Coming from Zürich, take the Zentrum exit then make a right at the traffic light. After the bridge make another right and follow the signs.

HOTEL DES BALANCES
Owner: Peter E. Büsser
Weinmarkt
CH-6000 Lucerne, Switzerland
Tel: (041) 418 28 28, Fax: (041) 418 28 38
57 rooms, Double: CHF 360–CHF 550
Open: all year, Credit cards: all major
56 km SW of Zürich, Train: 700 meters
Region: Lucerne
karenbrown.com/switzerland/balances.html

Although some tourists opt for a hotel with a lakefront setting, my heart remains with the Wilden Mann—an oasis of charm and hospitality snuggled in the ever-so-appealing medieval heart of Lucerne. Artistically arranged antiques of the finest quality are used throughout this delightful small hotel. The bedrooms too are beautifully decorated and each has its own personality. The ambiance is that of a private home rather than a large hotel. There are three dining rooms, each delightful in its own way. The Wilden Mann Stube is a French-style restaurant with rose tablecloths, candlelight, and, in cold weather, a cozy fire. This dining room has a special feature: on one of the walls there are three framed scenes depicting the Wilden Mann as it appeared in the mid-1800s. Upstairs there is another dining area—an outdoor garden terrace where tables are set for dining on warm summer days. However, my favorite place to dine is the Burgerstube, a charming, Swiss-country-style dining room with an ambiance of informality and warmth and wonderful wooden chairs—many of them antiques—set around the tables. *Directions:* Arriving from Interlaken, exit Luzern-Sud. Take the left lane and continue driving to Pilatusplatz (crossing). Pass under the house on the square, taking the lane to the right. After 100 meters turn right (Parkhaus Kesselturm). The hotel is next to this covered public parking.

ROMANTIK HOTEL WILDEN MANN
Owners: Ursula & Charles Zimmermann
Bahnhofstrasse 30
CH-6000 Lucerne, Switzerland
Tel: (041) 210 16 66, Fax: (041) 210 16 29
50 rooms, Double: CHF 330–CHF 430
Open: all year, Credit cards: all major
56 km SW of Zürich, Train: 500 meters
Region: Lucerne
karenbrown.com/switzerland/wildenmannhotel.html

The Romantik Hotel Ticino is located right at the heart of the historic section of Lugano on one of its charming little piazzas. Tucked just off the cobbled street, the hotel's entry is cozy and, just beyond, the inn opens up to an inner courtyard, which reflects the hotel's past history as a convent. Upstairs is a quiet guest lounge where you can relax and enjoy an evening drink. Because this is a very old building, bedrooms tend to be on the small side. If you desire more space, ask for a junior suite. My favorite guestrooms are the newly renovated ones, such as 27. These are very prettily decorated in pastel tones, and have the added bonus of air conditioning. Do not worry about street noise as rooms have double-paned windows and a great many have air conditioning. Just off the lobby is the hotel's restaurant, one of Lugano's most intimate and popular eating spots. As it is a favorite with locals, it is wise to make restaurant reservations when booking your room. The Hotel Ticino is a lovely, very old Tessin house that flourishes under the personal management and care of the gracious Buchmanns—a very special inn. *Directions:* From the autostrada, follow signposts for the center of the town until you see the hotel signpost to your right (before the train station). Continue straight into the pedestrian zone to the first square where you find the hotel on your right.

ROMANTIK HOTEL TICINO
Owners: Claire & Samuel Buchmann
Piazza Cioccaro 1
CH-6901 Lugano, Switzerland
Tel: (091) 922 77 72, Fax: (091) 923 62 78
18 rooms, Double: CHF 420–CHF 780
Open: Feb to Dec, Credit cards: all major
30 km N of Como, Train: 2-minute walk
Region: Ticino
karenbrown.com/switzerland/romantikhotelticino.html

Merlischachen   Swiss Chalet, Schloss Hotel, Château Golden Gate   Map: 2c

The Swiss Chalet was once the family home of the owners, Joseph and Ernst Seeholzer, and inside this marvelous old farmhouse, their family rooms have been converted to an intimate melange of dining nooks. Guestrooms in the original farmhouse are found at the top of a steep flight of stairs. Tucked under low ceilings, the accommodations are small, and simple in comfort and decor. Only a few have a private bath. In a newer, connecting building, a private dining room is found in what was once the house chapel, and upstairs a few rooms have been converted to guestrooms. We ventured to investigate two additional buildings that offer accommodation under the same ownership. The newly built Schloss Hotel across the street has a lakeside garden, antiques, armor, heavy beams, and wonderful large wooden doors that create an appealing, almost theatrical atmosphere. Guestrooms are modern in comfort, richly decorated, and many look out onto the lake. The Château Golden Gate, also newly constructed, is on the hillside above the other two buildings. Again, the use of armor, beams, and heavy doors give a feeling of an old castle. The guestrooms are large, lovely, and many enjoy wonderful views of the lake. There is also a rooftop terrace with spectacular views of the lake and distant mountains. *Directions:* Travel the road east from Lucerne towards Küssnacht. Merlischachen is just 12 km outside Lucerne and the hotel complex is on the main road.

SWISS CHALET
SCHLOSS HOTEL
CHÂTEAU GOLDEN GATE
Owner: Joseph Seeholzer
CH-6402 Merlischachen, Switzerland
Tel: (041) 854 54 54, Fax: (041) 854 54 66
71 rooms, Double: CHF 94–CHF 264
Open: all year, Credit cards: all major
12 km NE of Lucerne, Train: 5-minute walk
Region: Schwyz
karenbrown.com/switzerland/swisschalet.html

Le Vieux Manoir is constantly striving to improve its facilities and please its guests, so it justly deserves the very prestigious award of being named Gault Millau's Hotel of the Year 2000 for Switzerland. Located in the quietest of settings on the shore of Lake Murten, Le Vieux Manoir's beautiful exterior of weathered wood, little gables, high-pitched roofs, overhanging eaves, and whimsical chimneys complements an exquisite interior. The spacious bedrooms have either village or lake views, many have terraces, and all have luxurious decor and top-of-the-line marble bathrooms. A sumptuous breakfast buffet is set in the spacious breakfast room ringed by windows looking over the gardens to the lake. The conservatory, where lunch and dinner are served, offers an even more spectacular lake view. Dinner, either à la carte or table d'hôte, is an evening-long affair and if you grow short of conversation, you can always watch the artistry of the waiters as they serve one party after another with ballet-like precision. Of course, there's a high price to pay for such perfection. Le Vieux Manoir is a member of Relais & Châteaux. *Directions:* Exit the A1 autobahn at Murten and follow the hotel's signposts south to the adjacent little village of Meyriez.

LE VIEUX MANOIR AU LAC
Owner: Annelise Leu
Route de Lausanne
CH-3280 Meyriez-Murten, Switzerland
Tel: (026) 678 61 61, Fax: (026) 678 61 62
33 rooms, Double: CHF 195–CHF 385
Open: mid-Feb to mid-Dec, Credit cards: all major
34 km W of Bern, Train: 1 km
Relais & Châteaux
Region: Fribourg
karenbrown.com/switzerland/manoiraulac.html

The Carina-Carlton sits on the road facing Lake Lugano in the picturesque small village of Morcote, just a 20-minute drive south of Lugano. Across the street from the hotel is an outdoor restaurant perched on stilts over the lake, with flowers and a brightly striped awning adding even further enchantment to this dining haven. An inside dining room has a wood-beamed ceiling, white walls accented by green plants, and Oriental rugs covering its tiled floor. The breakfast buffet is set here but in fine weather guests usually eat on the adjacent patio. The bedrooms in front can be a bit noisy with the traffic on the street below, but they are still my favorites. Quieter rooms are found in the back, many looking out to the small pool snuggled in the upper terrace. I love room 35, a spacious room with excellent lake views. If you really want to splurge, room 45 is very special—a large, bright corner room with two balconies, one looking out over the tiled rooftops to the lake and the other overlooking the pool with a vista to the church. The Carina-Carlton is very convenient as a base in Switzerland's beautiful southern Lake District. You do not need a car—just board one of the ferries that ply the lake to the many quaint lakeside towns. *Directions:* Leave Lugano in the direction of Milan and Morcote is the first exit after the long tunnel. Follow the lakefront road for 5 km to the hotel. There is free parking at either end of the town.

HOTEL CARINA-CARLTON
Owners: Ingrid & Rudolf Tschannen
Via Cantonale
CH-6922 Morcote–Lugano, Switzerland
Tel: (091) 996 11 31, Fax: (091) 996 19 29
23 rooms, Double: CHF 180–CHF 310
Open: Mar to Nov, Credit cards: all major
6 km S of Lugano, Train: 6 km
Region: Ticino
karenbrown.com/switzerland/carinacarlton.html

Mürren is nestled on a high mountain shelf with the giant peaks of the Bernese Alps across the valley. From the village, massive granite walls drop straight down to the Lauterbrunnen Valley far below. There is no access by automobile—the only way to reach Mürren is by cable car from Stechelberg or by funicular from the Lauterbrunnen station. The Hotel Alpenruh is conveniently located next to the Schilthornbahn cable car, which begins at the valley floor at Stechelberg, stops in Mürren, and continues on to the Schilthorn. The hotel is not old, but is built in an attractive, low-rise chalet style. Wrapping around the front corner of the hotel is a large balcony, a favorite place for guests to gather on a sunny day to relish the view while enjoying a drink or perhaps lunch. Inside, the hotel is tastefully decorated in traditional style. Just to the left of the reception area is a cozy, pine-paneled lounge where guests can relax with a good book on a chilly day. The large dining room has a more modern look, but is softened by peasant-style paintings on paneled walls and brass gas lamp-style light fixtures. The bedrooms are fresh and attractive with typical Swiss pine furniture with a built-in headboard, table, and two chairs. Most of the bedrooms have balconies with glorious views of the mountains. *Directions:* From Interlaken, drive into the valley to Lauterbrunnen-Stechelberg. Park at Schilthornbahn and take the cable car to Mürren.

HOTEL ALPENRUH
Managers: Mr & Mrs Thomas Willem
CH-3825 Mürren, Switzerland
Tel: (033) 856 88 00, Fax: (033) 856 88 88
26 rooms, Double: CHF 210
Open: all year, Credit cards: all major
20 km S of Interlaken
Funicular from Lauterbrunnen: 5-min walk
Region: Bern
karenbrown.com/switzerland/alpenruh.html

Located just beyond the walls of the medieval town of Murten, directly on the banks of Lake Murten, the Hotel Schiff, which opened its doors as a hotel in 1767, enjoys a lovely waterside setting. The hotel is in the capable hands of Pierre Lehmann who oversees it with a gracious warmth and astute professionalism. With a multitude of dining rooms, a bar, and evening music, the Hotel Schiff has facilities that cater to groups ranging in size from 2 to 300 people. Often in the summer season you find a group visiting for lunch and a business function taking place, yet even when the place is bustling, the hotel also caters for the individual traveler. The 15 bedrooms are mostly traditional in their decor and many have tall windows that open up to glimpses of the lake through the trees. Rooms 4 and 5 have balconies. Guests can choose between a brasserie, French restaurant, or terrace for evening dining. A few minutes' walk finds you within the medieval walls of Murten. The ferry docks just in front of the hotel, tempting guests to take it to the interesting towns of Neuchâtel and Biel. *Directions:* Leave the Al autobahn at Murten and follow the hotel's signposts. There is plenty of metered parking around the hotel.

HOTEL SCHIFF
Owner: Pierre Lehmann
Direkt am See
CH-3280 Murten, Switzerland
Tel: (026) 670 27 01, Fax: (026) 670 35 31
15 rooms, Double: CHF 220–CHF 280
Open: all year, Credit cards: all major
31 km W of Bern, Train: 10-minute walk
Region: Fribourg
karenbrown.com/switzerland/hotelschiff.html

The Weisses Kreuz, located within the medieval walls of Murten, has been in the Bischoff family for over 80 years and demonstrates the warmth and special caring that comes only with owner-managed properties. The hotel consists of four very old buildings. One part of the hotel is a modern, white reception area with stairs leading up to a lovely dining room highlighted by a giant crystal chandelier. One wall is dominated by an oil painting of Swiss soldiers preparing to fight Charles the Bold, Duke of Burgundy, in a historically important battle that took place in Murten in 1476. If the Swiss army had lost, Switzerland might today belong to France. On warm days, meals are served outside on a magnificent balcony with a panoramic view of Lake Murten. Not only is the view stunning, but the food is outstanding. (The restaurant has the coveted Fish Medallion.) The majority of the rooms are across the street in old, charming, adjoining houses. Here the rooms come in every imaginable type of style and size ranging from vast rooms with antiques to doubles with contemporary decor. Rooms in the main building have the advantage of an elevator and several have French doors opening to balconies and wonderful lake views. *Directions:* Leave the A1 at Murten, drive through the city wall, and turn immediately right. Follow the road to the left and the hotel is on the right. Park to unload and the hotel will direct you to a car park.

HOTEL WEISSES KREUZ
Owners: Dr & Mrs Daniel Bischoff
Rathausgasse 31
CH-3280 Murten, Switzerland
Tel: (026) 670 26 41, Fax: (026) 670 28 66
27 rooms, Double: CHF 160–CHF 300
Open: Mar to Dec, Credit cards: all major
31 km W of Bern, Train: 500 meters
Region: Fribourg
karenbrown.com/switzerland/hotelweisseskreuz.html

As you enter through the Gothic archway into the Chasa Chalavaina, you slip back in time, with every nook and cranny breathing the history of yesteryear. In 1499, when the troops gathered in front of the inn prepared to battle the German Emperor, Maximilian, the Chasa Chalavaina was already at least 200 years old. From the beginning it was designed as an inn, as confirmed by the large stable where the coachmen sheltered their horses after their arduous journeys over the passes. The old stone floor of the entrance hall is worn smooth by the passage of countless guests. The Chasa Chalavaina has been restored with great respect for its past, with thick walls hung with farm instruments, doors with antique iron locks, old beams secured by wooden pegs, carved pine paneling wearing the patina of time, and rustic antiques galore. The inn has maintained the sturdy, simple, clean lines of the past while adding the conveniences of the present day. Delicious, home-cooked meals are served in the simple, pine-paneled dining room. Each of the guestrooms has its own personality: La Palantshotta has pine furniture and a large terrace tucked in under the eaves; La Stuietta, on the first floor, has its own private terrace; La Stuva del Preir has a deck overlooking the square in front of the hotel. The Chasa Chalavaina offers very basic accommodation and simple comfort. *Directions:* Müstair is just before the Italian border, 4 km northeast of Santa Maria.

HOTEL CHASA CHALAVAINA
Owner: Jonni Fasser
Plaza Grond
CH-7537 Müstair, Switzerland
Tel: (081) 858 54 68, Fax: none
15 rooms, Double: CHF 130–CHF 170
Open: all year
73 km NE of St. Moritz, Train to Zernez, 39 km by bus
Region: Graubünden
karenbrown.com/switzerland/chalavaina.html

I fell in love with this charming cluster of neighboring Engadine homes—one rust, one yellow, one mauve—sitting on Pontresina's main road. Once three individual houses dating from the 17th century, the buildings' communicating walls were torn down to accommodate one large hotel. The Steinbock is charming both inside and out. We entered off a garden courtyard terrace where guests were lingering over a late lunch, served by waitresses in handsome Tyrolean costume, into a cozy, welcoming ambiance of old pine and Alpine fabrics. Just off the reception is a lovely lounge, a large, open restaurant used for breakfast as well as dinner for pension guests and then there is a more intimate à-la-carte restaurant. We saw a number of guestrooms, which were all very pretty and simply decorated in light pines with white duvets topping the beds and patterned curtains and chairs. I absolutely loved number 10, a front corner room overlooking the garden terrace and opening onto the sound of the rushing river, which is unique in its lovely pine-paneled floor, walls, and ceiling. The hotel is owned by the Walther family who also operate the neighboring, very luxurious Walther Hotel, whose amenities such as indoor golf and swimming pool are available to guests of the Steinbock. *Directions:* From St. Moritz drive east on the 27 for 4 km and then south on the 29 for 4 km to Pontresina. The hotel is on the main street on the east side of town.

HOTEL STEINBOCK
Owner: Thomas Walther family
CH-7504 Pontresina, Switzerland
Tel: (081) 839 36 26, Fax: (081) 839 36 27
31 rooms, Double: CHF 220–CHF 365*
*Includes breakfast & dinner
Open: all year, Credit cards: all major
8 km outside of St. Moritz, Train to St. Moritz
Region: Graubünden
karenbrown.com/switzerland/steinbock.html

On the outskirts of cosmopolitan St. Moritz is a very pretty neighbor, Pontresina, whose buildings cluster on the hillside and look out to a sweeping ring of Alpine peaks. Standing proud above the main street of town, the Walther Hotel, built in a cream stone with a central entry tower and a few ornamental turrets, is as handsome inside as out. From the entryway an impressive wide hallway leads either to a spacious, elegant salon with many clustering seating arrangements or past the inviting hotel bar to a large open restaurant with dramatic high windows. This is the restaurant used for breakfast and pension guests. Step down round the corner to the Stuva Bella and you will enjoy the more intimate and cozy ambiance of the à-la-carte restaurant. I was able to see a number of guestrooms, reached up the grand central staircase. Rooms, which vary in size, look out either to the mountains or to the back hillside (these latter rooms are removed from any street noise). Some bedrooms have a sitting area, others enjoy beautiful pine paneling, and some have private balconies. Number 75 was one of my favorites with very pretty fabric, gorgeous paneling, and a small terrace. The hotel has a wonderful large swimming pool and a fitness and wellness center. *Directions:* From St. Moritz drive east on the 27 for 4 km and then south on the 29 for 4 km to Pontresina. The hotel sits on the main street on the east side of town.

WALTHER HOTEL
Owner: Thomas Walther family
Hauptstrasse, CH-7504 Pontresina, Switzerland
Tel: (081) 839 36 36, Fax: (081) 839 36 37
70 rooms, Double: CHF 310–CHF 730*
*Includes breakfast & dinner
Closed: Apr 21 to Jun 13, Oct to Dec, Credit cards: all major
8 km outside of St. Moritz, Train to St. Moritz
Relais & Châteaux
Region: Graubünden
karenbrown.com/switzerland/walther.html

The Rote Rose is the perfect inn with a superb setting on the knoll of a vineyard-laced hill. It is a meticulously restored, old timbered home in a beautiful walled village, with exquisite antiques and splendid views. Best of all though, the Rote Rose has as its owner Christa Schäfer, with her special qualities of warmth and hospitality—one of the finest hostesses I have ever met. And as if this is not enough to win your hearts, the walls of the inn are filled with the paintings of the renowned rose artist, Lotte Günthart, Christa's mother. Lotte Günthart's contribution to the world of roses has been so significant that a beautiful red rose is named for her. A short stroll away is Lotte Günthart's garden with over 500 varieties of roses. The Rote Rose has no restaurant, but serves goodies at happy hour. Every one of the rooms is a prize, but I think my favorite room remains Rose Dream—a suite with a sitting room, bedroom with canopy bed, dressing room, kitchenette, and windows overlooking the vineyards. Note: The newest addition to the Rote Rose is the beautifully restored 800-year-old Engelfrid House with five new suites. *Directions:* From Zürich airport follow the signs to Schaffhausen and exit at Bülach/Dielsdorf (West). From Dielsdorf, look for a sign for Regensberg and turn left up the hill. Turn right onto the cobblestone road. Drive through the Gasthaus Krone opening, turn right, and the Rote Rose is the second driveway on the right.

ROTE ROSE
Owner: Christa Schäfer
CH-8158 Regensberg, Switzerland
Tel: (01) 85 31 013, Fax: (01) 85 31 559
6 rooms, 8 suites, Double: CHF 220–CHF 410
Closed: Jan & Feb, Credit cards: all major
24 km N of Zürich, Train: 2 km, Airport: 20 mins
Region: Zürich
karenbrown.com/switzerland/roterose.html

The setting of the Gasthaus zum Gupf epitomizes Appenzell. Perched on the top of the highest rolling Alpine peak, this lovely timbered farmstead looks across the farmland of Appenzellerland to the distant Austrian and German peaks and to the glistening waters of the Bodensee. The Gasthaus zum Gupf boasts a justifiably serious restaurant with an exceptional menu featuring fresh produce and animals from the farm. There are two main dining rooms, the cozy Gupf Stube and the very elegant Alpstein Stube, and in warm weather tables are set on the outdoor terrace. The Gupf Stube, the smaller of the two restaurants, has a backdrop of light pines and looks out through delicate lace curtains to the surrounding countryside. The Alpstein Stube is more formal in its furnishings and has direct access to the incredible wine cellar. For the lucky few there are also six guestrooms upstairs—three singles, two doubles, and one suite, all with modern furnishings and commodious private bathrooms. The suite (room 5) overlooks the front acreage and enjoys the luxury of a sitting area and separate bath. Room 6, a double room, also overlooks the front, and room 7, a smaller double room, looks out through an angled ceiling window to views across Appenzellerland. Thanks to a Swiss friend for this recommendation! *Directions:* Located at the end of a single-lane road at the top of the town of Rehetobel, which is about 10 km east of St. Gallen.

GASTHAUS ZUM GUPF
Innkeeper: Emil Eberle family
Gupf 20
CH-9038 Rehetobel, Switzerland
Tel: (071) 877 11 10, Fax: (071) 877 15 10
6 rooms, Double: CHF 218–CHF 665
Closed: Feb & Aug, Sun & Mon in summer
Credit cards: all major
10 km E of St. Gallen, Train to St. Gallen
Region: Appenzell
karenbrown.com/switzerland/gupf.html

I have to thank Benno Meisser of the Hotel Meisser in Guarda for recommending this little gem of a hotel. At the end of a 13-kilometer unpaved road lies the village of S-Charl, a little piece of paradise tucked up against the towering Dolomites along a cascading river, right next to the Swiss National Park. The Ustaria (Restaurant) and Pensiun Crusch Alba & Alvetern is located within three of the village's only ten buildings. The cream-stucco houses are adorned with subtle exterior stenciling and wooden shutters in the lovely Engadine style. I was honestly surprised at the quality of accommodation and the dining options in the middle of what seemed like nowhere. Furnishings throughout reflect the style of the region, with lots of pine and plump duvets topping the beds. Modern bathrooms are gorgeous with hand-painted tiles. Bedrooms in the main house are the nicest, while four simple, rustic rooms with washbasin only are found in another building, Alvetern, which also houses a cozy stube offering light meals such as soups. The main restaurant for pension guests and the à-la-carte restaurant are both found in the main building and are lovely. A third charming building contains a large sitting room for guests. *Directions:* Traveling the 27 northeast from Zernez towards the Italian border, turn south at Vulpera following signs to S-Charl. You will travel along a challenging, unpaved road for 13 km (20 minutes) to the road's end.

CRUSCH ALBA & ALVETERN
Innkeeper: Sutter family
CH-7550 S-Charl, Switzerland
Tel: (081) 864 14 05, Fax: (081) 864 14 06
21 rooms, Double: CHF 100–CHF 180*
*Breakfast not included
Open: Jun 1 to Oct 20, Credit cards: all major
14 km E of Scuol, Train: 14 km
Region: Graubünden
karenbrown.com/switzerland/crusch.html

The Fletschhorn is a haven of tranquillity set on a forested hillside just outside Saas Fee overlooking the most breathtaking Alpine views. Yet this is far more than a hotel in a stunning location—it is a veritable haven for those who like their food not only to taste good but also to look good. Irma Dütsch and her brigade ensure that each dish looks like a stunning jewel: ravioli with truffles and mushrooms, lobster with white beans and seagrass, and a raspberry tart covered in a cloud of spun sugar were all too luscious to destroy. Small wonder that the Fletschhorn is one of the top eight restaurants in Switzerland. The same creativity displayed in the food is also found in the bedrooms, which come in two categories—bedrooms and junior suites. Junior suites are spacious affairs with open-plan bathrooms cleverly incorporated into the design of the room and balconies offering panoramic views. Bedrooms are smaller by comparison and more basic in their layout. Four rooms (31, 29, 34 and 35) boast fantastic views of the waterfalls and Alpine valley. Vivid colors and modern furnishings create a dramatic basis for the ever-changing collection of art that adorns the walls and open spaces. A 20-minute stroll from the heart of town. *Directions:* From Brig take the Zermatt road, branching to Saas Fee. Arriving in town, park in Lot A, unload, call the hotel, and the hotel's electric cart will come to meet you.

FLETSCHHORN
Owners: Irma & Jörg Dütsch
CH-3906 Saas Fee, Switzerland
Tel: (027) 957 21 31, Fax: (027) 957 21 87
15 rooms, Double: CHF 280–CHF 500*
*Includes breakfast & dinner
Closed: May to mid-Jun & Nov, Credit cards: all major
50 km SE of Zermatt, Train: call for free pick-up
Region: Valais
karenbrown.com/switzerland/fletschhorn.html

Nestled in a high mountain valley beneath a glacier and towering mountain peaks, Saas Fee is a traditional mountain village that has become a lively holiday resort. At the heart of the action you find one of its first hotels, the Romantik Hotel Beau-Site, a solid stone building constructed in 1893. The Zurbriggen family bought the hotel in 1944 and Urs is the third generation of his family to manage it. In more recent years the hotel has undergone a complete renovation that shows off the old stone walls and woodwork. This is particularly noticeable in the high-ceilinged public rooms—the sitting room with its exposed stone walls and heavy pine beams and the dining room all decked out with dark wood and furnished with intricately carved, old-world Swiss chairs. The hotel is a complete resort, with children's playroom, large swimming pool, and spa facilities. Bedrooms come in all shapes and sizes from simpler twin-bedded rooms to a grand suite with intricately carved furniture. Room 26 is an especially attractive suite and apartment 22, dating to the hotel's origins, is termed the Honeymoon Room. The hotel's broad terrace is a popular gathering spot serving traditional Swiss fare. *Directions:* From Brig take the Zermatt road, branching to Saas Fee. Arriving in town, park in parking lot A, unload your bags, call the hotel, and by the time you have taken your car to the parking garage the hotel's cart will be there to meet you.

ROMANTIK HOTEL BEAU-SITE
Owners: Marie-Jeanne & Urs Zurbriggen
CH-3906 Saas Fee, Switzerland
Tel: (027) 958 15 60, Fax: (027) 958 15 65
32 rooms, Double: CHF 336–CHF 526
Closed: mid-Apr to mid-Jun & Oct to Dec
Credit cards: all major
50 km SE of Zermatt, Train: call for free pick-up
Region: Valais
karenbrown.com/switzerland/beausite.html

Beautiful with its soft-yellow façade dressed with pretty shutters, the Grand Hotel Bella Tola is terraced on the hillside, fronted by a pretty garden and lawn, and looks out to the magnificence of the surrounding peaks and plunging valley. It is elegant and the Buchs-Favre family exude friendliness and hospitality. Bedrooms come in three categories: "classic", smaller tailored rooms with shower; "romantic", larger rooms furnished with lovely antiques accompanied by large bathrooms and balconies; and "superior", the same as romantic but a little larger. I was able to see every room, was charmed by them all, and noted all-too-many favorites: from 301, a lovely top corner room, to 306 with its own balcony, and 308, a smaller but charming corner room, to room 307 whose bathroom window gives a peek at the Matterhorn. In summer breakfast is served in the conservatory and for dinner you can choose between French cuisine in the conservatory or traditional Swiss fare in the cozy, traditional stubli. The village of St. Luc clings to the side of the valley, with skiing being the premier draw in winter and hiking and summer festivals in summer. Guests often take the funicular up the mountain to the observatory, and one of the most popular walks takes you to scale models of the planets. *Directions:* From Lausanne take the A9 autobahn south and then east to Sierre where you follow signs along the Val d'Anniviers, winding up the mountain for 20 km to Saint Luc.

GRAND HOTEL BELLA TOLA
Owners: Anne-Françoise & Claude Buchs-Favre
CH-3961 Saint Luc, Switzerland
Tel: (027) 475 14 44, Fax: (027) 475 29 98
32 rooms, Double: CHF 190–CHF 370
Open: Jan to Apr & mid-Jun to mid-Oct
Credit cards: MC, VS
22 km S of Sierre, Train to Sierre, 60 min bus to Saint Luc
Region: Valais
karenbrown.com/switzerland/bellatola.html

What a surprise it was after visiting Meierei Landgasthof on the edge of Lake Saint Moritz to walk into the Hotel Eden and find it is owned by the same family. The son, Maurizio, is busy managing the Meierei while his sister is busy at the Hotel Eden. Both seem to have the same cordial management style that is so frequently reflected when family is at the front desk. Although under the same ownership, there is no competition since each is entirely different. Whereas the Meierei Landgasthof is rustic in decor and well known for its restaurant, the Hotel Eden, which is well located in the heart of Saint Moritz, is a city hotel and serves only breakfast. As you enter the Eden, throw carpets warm the expanse of floor and straight ahead is an atrium, a sunny place to relax and enjoy the offering of afternoon tea. On your right is an old-fashioned, intimate parlor, furnished with rather formal antiques. Breakfast is served in a spacious downstairs dining room where each morning a bountiful buffet is artistically presented on an antique sleigh. The bedrooms are individual in decor and vary in size, decor, and view. Some are very motel-like and others have light knotty-pine furnishings. Room 138, a corner room with a bay window overlooking the lake, is particularly attractive. *Directions:* From the center of the village roundabout, access the hotel through the street in the direction of the parking garage. Continue straight, passing the cinema, and keep to the right.

HOTEL EDEN
Owner: Jehle-Degiacomi family
Via Veglia 12
CH-7500 Saint Moritz, Switzerland
Tel: (081) 830 81 00, Fax: (081) 830 81 01
35 rooms, Double: CHF 182–CHF 503
Open: Dec to Apr 15 & Jun 15 to Oct 15
Credit cards: MC, VS
63 km SW of Scuol, Train: 1 km
Region: Graubünden
karenbrown.com/switzerland/hoteledensw.html

From outside, the Hotel Languard looks like a typical patrician residence of wealthy Engadines with the lovely, regional, painted façade. Inside, this small family-owned and family-managed hotel has a warm country ambiance. Beyond the reception desk is an especially bright and cheerful breakfast room with large sunlit windows overlooking a panorama of Lake Saint Moritz. Here the theme is rustic country, with wooden pine tables and quaint carved wooden chairs. The bountiful breakfast buffet is laid out each morning on a fabulous, 17th-century carved wedding chest. There are only 22 guestrooms, each individually decorated, but all maintaining the same country feel with pine paneling and pine furniture. The large and very attractive corner rooms are the most expensive. Especially outstanding is room 9, which has not only handsomely carved antique wood paneling, but also a beautifully painted ceiling. There are splendid views of the lake and mountains from many of the rooms and a few even have a small balcony. The Hotel Languard is directly across a small square from the Hotel Eden. Both are small, personalized, family-run hotels. The Languard has a country ambiance, while the Eden is more formal. *Directions:* It is easy to get lost in the maze of one-way streets at the heart of town. Don't get discouraged—it is a small town and you will eventually arrive at Via Veglia.

HOTEL LANGUARD
Owner: Giovanni Trivella family
Via Veglia 14
CH-7500 Saint Moritz, Switzerland
Tel: (081) 833 31 37, Fax: (081) 833 45 46
22 rooms, Double: CHF 170–CHF 470
Open: Jun to Oct & Dec to Apr, Credit cards: all major
63 km SW of Scuol, Train: 1 km
Region: Graubünden
karenbrown.com/switzerland/languard.html

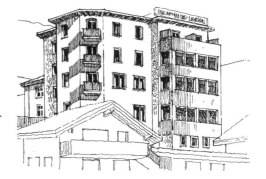

Although the address is Saint Moritz, the Meierei Landhotel is across the lake, with a pretty view back over the water to town. The hotel is actually an old farm whose origins date back to the 17th century when it was owned by a bishop. It was here that produce for the bishop's table was grown, tithes collected from the surrounding peasants, and beds kept ready for visiting dignitaries of the church. When the Degiacomi family bought the property, it had fallen into sad disrepair. They converted one wing into a very popular restaurant—a favorite place for those hiking around the lake to stop for lunch. The original part of the hotel is a white-stucco, two-storied building with brown shutters. The old restaurant wing, wrapped in weathered brown shingles, blends in very well. On sunny days, the most popular spot to dine is on the outdoor terrace, which is protected from the wind by a wall of glass. The main activity of the Meierei Landhotel is its restaurant, but there are also ten bedrooms furnished in a rustic pine decor. As you approach the main entrance, there is a children's playground to the right and an enticing corral with ponies. If you want to go into Saint Moritz for shopping, it is a pleasant 20-minute walk. Saint Moritz-Bad is also a 20-minute walk by a different path that loops around the lake. *Directions:* Take the Seepromenade on the northwest side of town (opposite the train station) around the lake.

MEIEREI LANDHOTEL
Owner: Maurizio Degiacomi
Via Dim Lej 52
CH-7500 Saint Moritz, Switzerland
Tel: (081) 833 20 60, Fax: (081) 833 88 38
10 rooms, Double: CHF 160–CHF 460
Open: Dec to Apr & Jun to Oct, Credit cards: all major
63 km SW of Scuol, Train: 1 km
Region: Graubünden
karenbrown.com/switzerland/meiereilandgasthof.html

The Domaine de Châteauvieux is just a 15-minute drive from the Geneva airport, a convenient hotel choice for a first or last night in Switzerland. It is difficult to comprehend that you are only a few miles west of a large city as you approach this 15th-century stone manor situated on the knoll of a hill laced with vineyards. You enter through the front gates into a courtyard with an antique wine press surrounded by an abundance of bright flowers. Inside the Domaine de Châteauvieux, there is a tasteful array of antiques gracefully intermingled with new furnishings to give a feeling of coziness and warmth. The emphasis is on dining that is truly gourmet. In the summer, meals are served out on the terrace overlooking the vineyards. On chilly days, meals are served in a very attractive dining room with old-world ambiance. The hotel is owned by the Chevrier family, and Philippe Chevrier is a superb chef who has justifiably earned two stars from Michelin for his fine restaurant. His wife, Bettina, is an extremely gracious hostess whose charm adds to the friendly atmosphere of the hotel. Since the Chevriers have purchased the hotel, they have been constantly refurbishing the comfortable guestrooms. *Directions:* Leave Geneva airport to the west in the direction of St. Genis. At Meyrin turn south and travel the few kilometers to Satigny.

ROMANTIK HOTEL DOMAINE DE CHÂTEAUVIEUX
Owner: Philippe Chevrier
Peney-Dessus
CH-1242 Satigny, Switzerland
Tel: (022) 75 31 511, Fax: (022) 75 31 924
17 rooms, Double: CHF 175–CHF 395
Closed: Jul 26 to Aug 11, Credit cards: all major
4 km W of Geneva airport, Train: 1 km, free pickup
Region: Geneva
karenbrown.com/switzerland/satigny.html

The Rheinhotel Fischerzunft is beautifully situated along the banks of the Rhine. The ferry leaves only a few steps from the hotel, making it a most convenient choice if you want to explore the river or just watch the boats go by. As you enter the hotel, an elegantly furnished dining room is to the left, and a sophisticated lounge furnished in muted colors to the right. There is a small staircase just off the hallway leading to a few guestrooms, each individually decorated—but all with a more modern, artistic decor. The rooms in front are termed suites and are the only rooms that face the river. Two of the suites are on the first floor and at water level, so views out the windows give the impression of being on a boat. There is only one suite on the second floor with views out through the dormer window. Until a century ago, the building used to house a fishermen's guild. It was converted to a restaurant and about 50 years ago it was expanded into a simple hotel. In recent years the hotel was purchased by the very talented Jaegers, who renovated the entire building—their exquisite taste is responsible for making the hotel so remarkably attractive. The outstanding, subtle, and fascinating Oriental flavors of the Fischerzunft's "East meets West" cuisine attracts guests from all over the world. The hotel is a member of Relais & Châteaux. *Directions:* The hotel is on the road that hugs the north side of town, on the west side of the river.

RHEINHOTEL FISCHERZUNFT
Owner: André Jaeger
Rheinquai 8
CH-8200 Schaffhausen, Switzerland
Tel: (052) 632 05 05, Fax: (052) 632 05 13
10 rooms, Double: CHF 280–CHF 440
Open: all year, Credit cards: all major
45 km N of Zürich, Train: 2 km
Relais & Châteaux
Region: Schaffhausen
karenbrown.com/switzerland/fischerzunft.html

We have received nothing but letters of praise for the Hotel Alpenrose, a long-time favorite in our guide. Michel Von Siebenthal and his wife, Carole, do an excellent job of carrying on the tradition of hospitality established by Michel's parents. Michel's mother, Monika, graciously greets guests and makes certain that everything runs smoothly. Although it has grown from a simple ski resort to a prestigious Relais & Châteaux hotel, the Alpenrose maintains the same warmth of welcome and value for money that it did when it was a much simpler property. Of course, it goes without saying that the food is delicious, whether you enjoy it in the delightful dining room or on the lovely terrace. Bedrooms generally are spacious affairs with lovely terraces or balconies enjoying stunning Alpine views across village rooftops. Several less expensive rooms face the street and are ideal for those who wish to experience this fine hotel and its delightful cuisine but who cannot afford a luxurious room. Whether you come to ski or to walk in the mountains, you will be enchanted with this lovely hotel. *Directions:* Schönried is 7 km north of Gstaad. Parking is in either the hotel's garage or an adjacent parking lot.

HOTEL ALPENROSE
Owner: Von Siebenthal family
CH-3778 Schönried–Gstaad, Switzerland
Tel: (033) 744 67 67, Fax: (033) 744 67 12
19 rooms, Double: CHF 380–CHF 700
Open: Dec to Oct, Credit cards: all major
7 km N of Gstaad, Train: 1 km
Relais & Châteaux
Region: Bern
karenbrown.com/switzerland/alpenrose.html

Originally a large private residence, the Hotel Margna was built in 1817 by Johann Josty who took advantage of a prime location, building his home on a small spit of land between two lakes. In the summertime there are countless paths along the lakefront or leading up to imposing mountain peaks, while in the winter this is an Alpine and cross-country skiers' paradise. Johann Josty's manor is now a beautiful hotel with gracious touches of sophistication—warm, cream-colored walls, antique accents such as an old sleigh laden with flowers, and Oriental rugs. There are several lounges, a grill restaurant with an open fireplace, a basement fondue restaurant (open only in winter months), a second dining room, the Stuva, a cozy, wood-paneled room original to the hotel, and a new garden terrace that is popular for both breakfast and lunch. The hotel has game rooms, a whirlpool, and steam bath. Each guestroom is delightful but I especially loved number 25, which enjoys views of lake and mountain through three large, arched windows. Golfers will be happy to know that the Margna has its own six-hole course and resident pro. Those on a budget should inquire about the newer wing of less expensive rooms. *Directions:* From St. Moritz travel south to Silvaplana and then 6 km south of Silvaplana cross over to a small peninsula dividing the Silvaplaner and Silser Sees to the tiny hamlet of Sils-Baselgia and the hotel.

HOTEL MARGNA
Managers: Regula & Andreas Ludwig
CH-7515 Sils–Baselgia, Switzerland
Tel: (081) 838 47 47, Fax: (081) 838 47 48
68 rooms, Double: CHF 420–CHF 700*
*Includes breakfast & dinner
Open: mid-Jun to mid-Oct & mid-Dec to mid-Apr
Credit cards: MC, VS
12 km S of St. Moritz, Postal bus from St. Moritz: 12 km
Region: Graubünden
karenbrown.com/switzerland/margna.html

The village of Sils-Maria is idyllic, nestled on a strip of land dividing two mountain-bound lakes. The Pensiun Privata is a charming inn, offering very reasonably priced accommodation and some of the region's most gracious hospitality. Family-run, the pretty, four-story, beige building with brown shutters is located on a small village square. Just to the left of the building is the gathering place for the colorful horse-drawn carriages that take guests into beautiful Val Fex. The hotel is strategically located for hiking—just outside the door, trails lead off in every direction: up into the mountains, into the meadows, around the lakes, and along the rushing creek. This is a pretty inn and I love its comfortable ambiance with crisp white linens, fresh flowers, and endless thoughtful touches. The flagstone entrance with a reception counter opens onto two cozy lounges. A hallway leads to an especially attractive, spacious dining room with windows overlooking the back garden with some lovely sitting places and a sheltered veranda. The dining room has a paneled ceiling, an antique armoire, pine chairs, and fresh flowers everywhere. The dinner is a four-course menu and the food is excellent. Ursula, Dumeng, and their daughters make this a very special place. *Directions:* From St. Moritz travel south to Silvaplana and after 4 km turn left at the traffic sign for Sils-Maria. You will find the Pensiun Privata right on the village square.

HOTEL PENSIUN PRIVATA
Owners: Ursula & Dumeng Giovanoli
CH-7514 Sils–Maria, Switzerland
Tel: (081) 832 62 00, Fax: (081) 832 62 01
25 rooms, Double: CHF 260–CHF 330*
*Includes breakfast & dinner, Meals for hotel guests only
Open: Dec 13 to Apr 18 & Jun 5 to Oct 10
Credit cards: all major
10 km S of St. Moritz, Postal bus from St. Moritz: 10 km
Region: Graubünden
karenbrown.com/switzerland/hotelpensiunprivata.html

The Romantik Hotel Al Cacciatore is a gem—a tiny hotel that has everything your heart could desire: a quaint village setting, stunning mountain scenery, a delightful restaurant, tasteful decor, and pretty antique furnishings. Adding the final touch of perfection is your charming hostess, Silvia Cafiero, who welcomes guests like friends and lavishes personal attention upon them. Her grandfather came from this tiny village, which she came to love as a child. Many years later, she and her Italian husband, Luigi, left their estate in southern Italy, moved to Soazza, and bought a simple restaurant from one of Silvia's relatives. Then, at an age when most people think of retiring and just enjoying a quiet life, they embarked upon a huge endeavor: totally renovating the property, redoing the restaurant, adding guestrooms, decorating every corner to perfection, and opening a superb little inn. The hotel is housed within a cluster of very old buildings constructed around intimate courtyards. Care was taken to enrich the original architectural features while adding every modern comfort. When the renovation was finished, Silvia decorated the hotel with handsome family antiques and her personal art collection, giving the hotel a warm, homelike ambiance. *Directions:* The hotel is in the heart of Soazza, which is located just off the A13, 20 minutes north of Bellinzona, en route to the San Bernardino Pass.

ROMANTIK HOTEL AL CACCIATORE   *New*
Owners: Silvia Cafiero & Marca de Donatz
Piazzetta
CH-6562 Soazza, Switzerland
Tel: (091) 831 1820, Fax: (091) 831 1979
17 rooms, Double: CHF 230–CHF 270
Closed: mid-Jan to mid-Mar, Credit cards: all major
30 km N of Bellinzona, Train: 5 km
Region: Ticino
karenbrown.com/switzerland/cacciatore.html

La Soglina is a gem of a hotel in an incredibly picturesque village, high on a shelf-like terrace overlooking the Bregaglia Valley. The hotel is owned by the Nass-Schumacher family. Mr Nass, originally from Strasbourg, France, is the talented chef in charge of the kitchen. His gracious wife was born in Soglio. The hotel is spread over three buildings in this small village—two stand together at the top and outskirts of town and one is just at its entrance. The reception is located in the newer of the two buildings at the top, along with a recently built restaurant and ten guestrooms. Clean and simple in their decor, the bedrooms are spacious, with Berber-style carpets, whitewashed walls, and sturdy, light-pine furniture. The bathrooms are modern. The restaurant is beautiful with its pine furnishings and carved ceilings. Tables overflow onto an expanse of terrace and enjoy absolutely spectacular vistas. An underground passageway connects the two buildings—the second houses guestrooms and a fitness center with sauna and solarium. Although the rooms are nice and the meals hearty, the outstanding feature of La Soglina is its location. Request one of the most expensive rooms with a view balcony, then settle in for a long stay. You will come home with memories of walks through fields of flowers and mountain panoramas that are almost too perfect to be true. *Directions:* Soglio is located just a few kilometers up a winding road from the 37 (60 km SW of St. Moritz).

🍵 🏊 💳 ☎ 🏋 👫 P 🍴

LA SOGLINA
Owners: E. & R. Nass-Schumacher
CH-7610 Soglio, Switzerland
Tel: (081) 822 16 08, Fax: (081) 822 15 94
33 rooms, Double: CHF 130–CHF 150
Closed: Nov, Credit cards: all major
60 km SW of St. Moritz
Postal bus St. Moritz to Promontogno to Soglio
Region: Graubünden
karenbrown.com/switzerland/soglina.html

The Hotel Krone, a 13th-century residence, is in the fascinating walled medieval town of Solothurn. The cozy exterior leaves nothing to be desired: a pale-pink stuccoed building, muted green shutters, and windowboxes overflowing with red geraniums. The location, too, is perfect—facing onto the colorful main square, just opposite Saint Ursen Cathedral. The reception area is more formal than the exterior would indicate, but the dining room has an inviting country-inn atmosphere and fresh flowers are plentiful on the tables. At the top of the stairwell is a large room often used for private parties. There is also a relaxing bar, perfect for a welcome drink. Tables are set outside in good weather for light meals. The bedrooms are all very similar in decor, with copies of Louis XV furniture, which blend nicely with genuine antiques. The more deluxe rooms are especially large and have spacious bathrooms with tubs so big you can almost go swimming in them. Since our original stay at the Hotel Krone, all of the bedrooms have been renovated, and now all of the double rooms are spacious in the old section of the inn. The smaller rooms are in the new addition and are used as singles. *Directions:* Solothurn is located halfway between Basel and Bern on the River Aare and Route 12.

HOTEL KRONE
Owners: Marie-Therèse & Gerald Dörfler-Aerni
Hauptgasse 64
CH-4500 Solothurn, Switzerland
Tel: (032) 622 44 12, Fax: (032) 622 37 24
42 rooms, Double: CHF 240–CHF 300
Open: all year, Credit cards: all major
76 km S of Basel, Train: 700 meters
Region: Solothurn
karenbrown.com/switzerland/hotelkronesw.html

The Hotel Rheinfels, a beige building with brown shutters, sits directly on the banks of the Rhine as it flows through the storybook-perfect medieval village of Stein am Rhein. In fact, the hotel is so close to the Rhine that the geranium-festooned dining terrace actually stretches out over the water. The restaurant, where you register, seems to be the focal point of the Hotel Rheinfels, but a wide staircase, lined with family portraits, leads up to an attractive lounge decorated with several antique armoires, tables, paintings, and suits of armor. All of the guestrooms are very similar both in decor and size, and all have been completely renovated. Although the bedrooms' built-in furniture is clean and functional, a traditional mood is achieved through the use of floral carpeting in shades of rose, pretty wallpaper, and color-coordinated fabrics on the chairs and sofabeds. Every room has its own attractively tiled bathroom. The bedrooms are exceptionally spacious, bright, and cheerful. All rooms but one enjoy windows overlooking the river and it, by contrast, looks out over the medley of town roofs. The family has converted what was their mother's riverside apartment into a spacious rental—an exceptional value. (It even shares a pier with the swans.) *Directions:* Stein am Rhein is approximately 18 km east of Schaffhausen on the Untersee. The Hotel Rheinfels is located right on the water, the first house after the bridge on the left side.

HOTEL RHEINFELS
Owner: Edi Schwegler-Wick
CH-8260 Stein am Rhein, Switzerland
Tel: (052) 741 21 44, Fax: (052) 741 25 22
17 rooms, Double: CHF 180–CHF 250, (Apt. CHF 250)
Open: Mar 10 to Dec 12, Credit cards: all major
18 km E of Schaffhausen, Boat dock: 100 meters
Region: Schaffhausen
karenbrown.com/switzerland/hotelrheinfels.html

The deluxe Schloss Hotel Chastè is in a tiny village (just a cluster of farmhouses) in a gorgeous high meadow of the glorious Engadine Valley, bounded by the soaring peaks of the majestic Dolomites. Completing the idyllic scene is the picturesque Tarasp Castle crowning a nearby hill and a small lake in the flower-filled meadow. Until the turn of the century, the hotel was a farmhouse, and has incredibly been in the same family since it was built in 1480. When Tarasp Castle was being renovated in 1912, Anton Pazeller, the grandfather of the present owner, opened a small restaurant to accommodate tourists coming to see the castle. His grandson, your gracious host, Rudolf Pazeller, trained as a chef and returned home to expand the hotel and add a gourmet restaurant. The façade is in the traditional Engadine style, painted white and accented with intricate designs. Pink geraniums cascade from every windowbox. Inside, you find beautiful carved-wood paneling throughout and country-style furnishings, which create a charming, rustic ambiance. The bedrooms are individual in decor, but all have a cozy look with furniture made from various woods native to the Engadine. This is a lovely inn in an idyllic setting. Just steps from the hotel, walking paths lead off in every direction. *Directions:* From St. Moritz, follow the sign for Scuol. Before Scuol, follow the sign for Tarasp-Vulpera, 4 km up the hill. There is a sign for the hotel in Tarasp-Fontana.

SCHLOSS HOTEL CHASTÈ
Owners: Daniela & Rudolf Pazeller
CH-7553 Tarasp, Switzerland
Tel: (081) 861 30 60, Fax: (081) 861 30 61
20 rooms, Double: CHF 400–CHF 580
Open: Jan to Mar & Jun to Oct, Credit cards: all major
70 km NW of St. Moritz, Train to Scuol, bus to Tarasp
Relais & Châteaux
Region: Graubünden
karenbrown.com/switzerland/schlosschaste.html

If you want to combine resort-style living on the lake and still be within an hour of Lucerne by boat or half an hour by car, then the Park Hotel Vitznau might be your cup of tea. It has an ideal, beautiful parklike setting directly on the banks of Lake Lucerne. This is not a rustic hotel in any way. Rather, it is sophisticated, with all the amenities that you would expect from a deluxe establishment—a large heated indoor-outdoor swimming pool, sauna, steam bath, table tennis, bicycles, and a motorboat for water skiing or excursions. The lakeside setting also allows sailing, swimming, and fishing. The building is like a castle, with turrets, towers, gables, and many nooks and crannies. A beautiful lawn surrounded by gardens runs down from the hotel to the edge of the lake where a promenade follows the contours of the lakefront. The setting is one of such bliss that it is hard to believe you are so close to the city of Lucerne. Inside, the lobby, lounge areas, and dining room are beautifully decorated with combinations of wood beams, fireplaces, Oriental rugs on gleaming hardwood floors, green plants, and antique accents. *Directions:* From Zürich airport take the highway in the direction of Lucerne, exit at Rotkreuz to the highway for Schwyz, then exit in Küssnacht and travel south along the lake to Vitznau.

PARK HOTEL VITZNAU
Manager: Peter Bally
Kantonsstrasse
CH-6354 Vitznau, Switzerland
Tel: (041) 399 60 60, Fax: (041) 399 60 70
104 rooms, Double: CHF 570–CHF 2000
Open: mid-Apr to mid-Oct, Credit cards: all major
25 km E of Lucerne, Boat from Lucerne: 25 km
Region: Lucerne
karenbrown.com/switzerland/vitznau.html

The Hotel Villa Maria, above the Engadine Valley, sits on the road from Bad Scuol as it winds up into the hills toward the picturesque Tarasp Castle. Although the road loops around the hotel, there is an ornately tended garden with decorative gnomes and a "pitch and put" green along the side. The 100-year-old inn, painted a pale yellow with intricately carved wooden balconies and brown shutters, has a Victorian flair which is given a Swiss touch by the traditional boxes overflowing with geraniums hung at every window. Inside, there is a country ambiance—carved pine ceilings, intricate paneling, pine furniture, antiques, and fresh flowers abound. The bedrooms are attractive. All have light-pine furniture offset by the same provincial-print fabrics used in the window coverings. Everything is fresh and new and very pretty. For guests who stay three days, a demi-pension plan is available, with breakfast and dinner included in the room rate. For these guests there is a bright, cheerful dining room overlooking the back garden. In addition, on the street level there is a gourmet restaurant with beamed ceilings, thick planked-wood walls, many antiques, a fireplace, and a charming fondue restaurant off the garden. The Villa Maria is in a wooded area with walking trails feathering off in every direction. *Directions:* Traveling east on the 27, turn south just before Scuol and cross the river to Vulpera.

HOTEL VILLA MARIA
Owner: Erich Jaeger
CH-7552 Vulpera, Switzerland
Tel: (081) 864 11 38, Fax: (081) 864 91 61
15 rooms, Double: CHF 196–CHF 300
Open: May 20 to Nov & Christmas to Easter
Credit cards: all major
63 km NE of St. Moritz, Train to Bad Scuol, bus to hotel
Region: Graubünden
karenbrown.com/switzerland/villamariasw.html

Dorly and Urs-Peter Geering are excellent hoteliers, shining lights of Switzerland's most highly regarded profession. The Beau Rivage on the shore of Lake Lucerne is their home, so one of them is always on hand and the warmth they offer guests is echoed by the entire staff from the porter to the maitre d'. To be certain that guests have the opportunity to see everything in the area, the Geerings have arranged for a member of the local tourist office to come several times a week to discuss where to go and what to see. Of course, you must take the ferry to Lucerne and the gondola up to Rigi! However, with the Beau Rivage's unsurpassed lakeside location, it is tempting to while away the hours soaking in the view of the boat activity on the mountain-backed lake and taking dips in the pool and lunch on the shaded patio. Naturally, you should request a bedroom with a lake view—some have spacious terraces, others snug balconies. However, you get the best value for money in the spacious rooms under the eaves (no balcony or terrace). *Directions:* From Zürich exit the N4 at Küssnacht and follow the signs along Lake Lucerne to where you find the Hotel Beau Rivage on your right.

HOTEL BEAU RIVAGE
Owners: Dorly & Urs-Peter Geering
Gottardstrasse 6
CH-6353 Weggis, Switzerland
Tel: (041) 392 79 00, Fax: (041) 390 19 81
41 rooms, Double: CHF 220–CHF 420
Open: Apr to Oct, Credit cards: all major
20 km E of Lucerne, Train to Lucerne & boat to Weggis
Region: Lucerne
karenbrown.com/switzerland/beaurivage.html

The Hotel Alte Post, an old coaching inn, is a charming country hotel on the road between the international resort of Gstaad and the magnificent lake district of Interlaken. The hotel backs onto the rushing waters of the River Simme. You enter the hotel from the street into a small, informal entry. On one side is a simple country restaurant decorated with pine tables and lovely painted beams and on the other side is a more formal restaurant, elegant in decor. At the back of the inn is a very informal dining area whose tables are set against windows with views of the river. When the weather cooperates, tables are also set outside on a terrace. Nine of the hotel's ten guestrooms are located on the top floor (the other is on the floor below). All are very rustic in their decor, with wood-paneled walls and ceilings and country antiques—very reminiscent of a country "ferme auberge". The sound of the road traffic is diminished by the time it reaches the top floor and any sound that could be heard is drowned out by the rushing river. Six of the bedrooms have a private bathroom with shower, two have a private bathroom with tub, and two are equipped with a sink only. The rooms are comfortably furnished and very reasonable in price. First-class cuisine is prepared by the owner and chef, Herr Brazerol. *Directions:* Weissenburg is right on the river, approximately 20 km east of Spiez and Lake Thun. The Alte Post is on the main road.

HOTEL ALTE POST
Owners: Mr & Mrs Franz Brazerol
CH-3764 Weissenburg im Simmental, Switzerland
Tel: (033) 783 15 15, Fax: (033) 783 15 78
10 rooms, Double: CHF 100–CHF 170
Closed: Apr & Oct, Credit cards: all major
30 km NE of Gstaad, Train: 10-minute walk
Region: Bern
karenbrown.com/switzerland/hotelaltepost.html

When at the end of the 19th century word spread of the incredible beauty of the Alps, sporty travelers began to find their way to Wengen. At that time Wengen was merely a cluster of wooden farmhouses clinging to a mountain shelf high above the Lauterbrunnen Valley. In 1881, Friedrich and Margaritha Feuz-Lauener (great-grandparents of the present owner Paul von Allmen) gambled on tourism and built the Alpenrose, the village's first hotel. Through the years, the hotel has expanded, but the traditional warmth of hospitality remains. Paul and his gracious Scottish wife, Margaret, make all guests feel very special. This is not a fancy hotel, but has great heart. The lounges are cozily decorated with a homey ambiance. The dining room is large and becomes a meeting place where everyone has their own table for dinner each night—a time when guests share their day's adventures and often become friends. Paul von Allmen is the chef and the set dinner menu features good home cooking. Most of the bedrooms have been completely renovated and are fresh and pretty with light-pine furniture. Request a south-facing room with a balcony to capture the splendor of the Jungfrau. *Directions:* Cars are not allowed in Wengen. A hotel porter meets guests at the station or if you have just a little luggage, you might want to walk the short distance to the hotel. A town map is available at the train station.

HOTEL ALPENROSE – COVER PAINTING
Owner: Paul von Allmen family
CH-3823 Wengen, Switzerland
Tel: (033) 855 32 16, Fax: (033) 855 15 18
50 rooms, Double: CHF 246–CHF 324*
*Includes breakfast & dinner
Open: mid-Dec to mid-Apr & May to Oct
Credit cards: all major
16 km S of Interlaken, Train: 7-minute walk
Region: Bern
karenbrown.com/switzerland/hotelalpenrose.html

As your train pulls into Wengen (coming by train is the only access), you will see the Hotel Regina perched on the knoll above the station. If you call ahead, the hotel porter will be there to meet you. I saw one cart pull away brimming with children, parents, luggage, and a dog. When you enter the hotel, you will probably be reminded of one of the British resorts so popular at the turn of the last century. The downstairs has large, rambling lobbies punctuated with small seating areas where chairs encircle game tables, and a huge fireplace surrounded by overstuffed chairs—it all looks very Swiss-British. The Chez Meyer dining room is very special, intimate in size, its walls hung with family photos—generations of Meyers who have operated hotels in Kandersteg and now in Wengen, Switzerland's beautiful mountain towns. Notice the chairs that have brass tags of the 11 family members who are always welcome at the Regina. The decor is lovely, and the Meyer family is extremely gracious and happily welcomes guests who return year after year—a tradition for many. The view from the Regina is so stunning that everything else pales in significance. Ask for a room with a balcony—when you're outside, you feel as if you can touch the mountain peaks. *Directions:* Wengen is 16 km up the valley from Interlaken. Cars are not allowed in this mountain village so you have to park at the train station in Lauterbrunnen and then take the cog train up to Wengen.

HOTEL REGINA
Owners: Ariane & Guido Meyer
CH-3823 Wengen, Switzerland
Tel: (033) 855 15 12, Fax: (033) 855 15 74
90 rooms, Double: CHF 230–CHF 440*
*Includes breakfast & dinner
Open: all year, Credit cards: all major
16 km S of Interlaken, Train: 3-minute walk
Region: Bern
karenbrown.com/switzerland/regina.html

In the small town of Worb, just a few kilometers east of Bern, sits the Hotel Löwen. This pretty inn, which dates back to 1547, is positioned at the junction of two busy streets but, even so, radiates an immense amount of charm. Ursula or Hans-Peter Bernhard is usually on hand to welcome guests for the Hotel Löwen is their home, with their family living upstairs. A series of cozy, traditional dining rooms occupies the ground floor—one is reserved for non-smokers and it is here that breakfast is served, though during the summer, guests usually eat outside in the shade of the sycamore trees. Just off the garden is a bowling alley and Herr Bernhard is always happy to give a demonstration of Swiss bowling. He is also happy to share his other hobbies: his corkscrew and wine collections. While the restaurant has a list of 50 to 60 wines, Hans-Peter has a far larger selection in his nearby shop. The spotless but simply decorated bedrooms all have small refrigerators containing complimentary beers, water, and snacks. My favorite room was number 14 with its window opening up to the church and its intricate, paper-cut pictures on the walls. The Hotel Löwen is just 200 meters from the train station, making it a perfect location for a day trip to Bern. From Worb the road winds up into the Emmental Valley. *Directions:* From Bern take the A6 towards Interlaken, exit for Langau and drive 10 km to Worb. The hotel is in the center of town.

HOTEL LÖWEN
Owner: Hans-Peter Bernhard
Enggisteinstrasse 3
CH-3076 Worb, Switzerland
Tel: (031) 839 23 03, Fax: (031) 839 58 77
13 rooms, Double: CHF 165–CHF 175
Open: all year, Credit cards: all major
8 km E of Bern, Train: 200 meters
Region: Bern
karenbrown.com/switzerland/hotellowen.html

Sitting high above Zermatt, the Grand Hotel Schönegg has a panoramic view of the towering Matterhorn across the rooftops of the town. In spite of its hillside location you don't have to climb to reach your lofty retreat for the hotel has an elevator, accessed through a grotto-like passageway, which whisks you up from the town. The classic chalet façade is matched by a classic interior, with heavy pine beams and ornate plasterwork ceilings in the public areas and traditional furnishings in the bedrooms. Of course, capturing the view of the Matterhorn is the name of the game in Zermatt and the Schönegg offers many possibilities: from the spacious terrace, the dining room, and a great many of the bedrooms. Bedrooms are found on two floors below and two above the reception area. The majority of rooms enjoy balconies and views of the Matterhorn. The most dramatic is the south-facing suite 604, accessed by its own private stairway and profiting from an expanse of deck. Two of my favorite rooms (502 and 503) were in the superior category, both cozily set under the eaves with magnificent views. Service and food are exceptional and the price for one of Zermatt's loveliest hotels is surprisingly one of the town's best values. *Directions:* Park you car by the train station in Tasch, take the train to Zermatt, and your hotel golf cart will be waiting at the station.

GRAND HOTEL SCHÖNEGG
Owner: Metry-Julen family
CH-3920 Zermatt, Switzerland
Tel: (027) 966 34 34, Fax: (027) 966 34 35
36 rooms, Double: CHF 446–CHF 770
Closed: Oct, Nov & May, Credit cards: all major
A short walk from heart of town, Train: 10-min walk
Relais & Châteaux
Region: Valais
karenbrown.com/switzerland/schonegg.html

To stay at the Riffelalp, sitting high on a plateau above the city of Zermatt, is to enjoy an elegant resort oasis and unobstructed views of the Matterhorn in a spectacular Alpine setting. During a recent renovation the original four-story, cream-stucco hotel was gutted and the ambiance of a gorgeous Alpine chalet was created using beautiful Alpine pines, which will characteristically darken with age, for much of the flooring and walls, and even as the basis for the hand-painted ceilings. A welcome cocktail is offered in the attractive bar with its large open fireplace and many cozy sitting areas. The main Alexander Restaurant is large but intimate seating areas are created by partitioning off tables and booths, and tables spill out onto the terrace for summer breakfasts or lunches. The lovely guestrooms, all with modern bathroom conveniences and Jacuzzis, have a decor of beautiful Alpine pines and fabrics and most enjoy views of the Matterhorn. Once you arrive in this idyllic but isolated setting you will not want to leave so the hotel provides many attractions and amusements including an underground bowling alley (nominal charge), wine tasting, and paragliding. Reservations must be made in advance. Summer is easier to reserve than winter when they are booked for months ahead. *Directions:* Take the 20-minute cog-wheel train ride from Zermatt.

RIFFELALP RESORT
Director: Hans Jorg Walther
Riffelalp, CH-3920 Zermatt, Switzerland
Tel: (027) 966 05 55, Fax: (027) 966 05 50
63 rooms, Double: CHF 540–CHF 1160*
*Includes breakfast & dinner
Closed: Apr 13 to Jun 19 & Sep 25 to Dec 11
Credit cards: all major
Above Zermatt, Train: Cog wheel train from Zermatt
Region: Valais
karenbrown.com/switzerland/riffelalp.html

A cascade of colorful flowers decks every inch of the balconies of the Hotel Julen at the height of summer—a lovely sight. This hotel, owned and managed by Daniela and Paul Julen, is well located, just across the bridge and river from the heart of Zermatt. Inside, the decor is surprisingly modern with bold designs and strong colors. Just off the entry, stools around the bar as well as leather sofas in front of the cozy fireplace attract many guests—the ambiance is one of relaxation and friendliness. Settle on the patio and watch the changing moods of the Matterhorn, enjoy a salad-bar lunch or an à-la-carte dinner in the dining room. Another option is a traditional, romantic meal in the Schäferstube ("lamb room"), a romantic, old-world dining room. Bedrooms vary in size from elegant suites to more standard twin-bedded rooms. Paneled in 100-year-old spruce wood and furnished with traditional light-pine furniture, each guestroom has green silk drapes and contrasting striped carpets. The three choice rooms (107, 108, and 109) all open onto an expanse of balcony and unobstructed views of the Matterhorn. The fitness center offers everything that you expect to find at a luxurious resort, including a swimming pool with water jets, an incredible weight room, and a sauna. *Directions:* Park your car by the train station in Täsch, take the train to Zermatt, and your hotel golf cart will be waiting at the station.

ROMANTIK HOTEL JULEN
Owners: Daniela & Paul Julen
CH-3920 Zermatt, Switzerland
Tel: (027) 966 76 00, Fax: (027) 966 76 76
32 rooms, Double: CHF 194–CHF 464*
*Includes breakfast & dinner
Open: all year, Credit cards: all major
A short walk from the heart of town, Train: 5-min walk
Region: Valais
karenbrown.com/switzerland/romantikhoteljulen.html

The Schlosshotel Tenne, just a two-minute walk from the main Zermatt rail terminal, is one of the few hotels in Zermatt to incorporate into its structure a very old wooden chalet. Part of the hotel is of more modern construction but the old and the new have been blended well. The hotel is owned by an old Zermatt family, the Perrens. The Tenne is managed by the Perrens' daughter Sonja and Werner Kradolfer whose gracious hospitality makes guests feel very welcome. The hotel has a modern, Swiss art-deco theme—walls, pillars, and carvings all have this motif. In the chalet are five suites termed "rustic" rooms because of their blond carved paneling. Each has a separate sitting room (with fireplace) and bedroom. Several face the Matterhorn with the Gornegrat cog railway station in between. All the bedrooms have a bathroom with whirlpool tub. The hotel usually quotes half-pension rates at a CHF 30 supplement per person above the bed-and-breakfast rates. This is a very good value for money as the food is of a very high standard. One can choose to dine in the larger dining room or in the cozy, rustic stube. Ask about the great skiing and hiking packages. *Directions:* Park you car by the train station in Tasch and take the train to Zermatt. As you leave the train station, you will see the arched sign for the Schlosshotel Tenne opposite, next to the Gornegrat cog railway station.

SCHLOSSHOTEL TENNE
Owner: Sonja Biner-Perren
Managers: Sonja Biner-Perren & Werner Kradolfer
CH-3920 Zermatt, Switzerland
Tel: (027) 966 44 00, Fax: (027) 966 44 05
38 rooms, Double: CHF 300–CHF 600*
*Includes breakfast & dinner
Open: Dec 15 to mid-Oct, Credit cards: all major
At the heart of Zermatt, Train: 50 meters
Region: Valais
karenbrown.com/switzerland/tenne.html

The Seiler family is an integral part of Zermatt. It was back in the mid-1800s when Alexander Seiler ventured into the hotel business with the first hotel in Zermatt—the Monte Rosa. The following generations have continued in the business of hospitality and expanded the family enterprise to include the Mont Cervin, the finest, most elegant hotel in Zermatt. As you enter the hotel it is hard to believe that such a chic resort could be situated in a mountain village. The ceilings are high, with lovely paneling in some areas and wood beams in others, and there are Oriental carpets, fine antique furniture, and flowers everywhere. Converted from what was once a garden courtyard, the Rendezvous bar is a welcoming place to enjoy a drink and the afternoon piano bar. The main dining room, painted in pretty, soft yellow and blue, has a tranquil formality combined with a reputation for gourmet food and exquisite service. You find more casual dining in the pine-paneled bar. Guestrooms are located in four buildings and run the gamut from deluxe Alpine-style apartments to traditional double bedrooms. Naturally, the premier rooms have a heart-stopping view of the towering Matterhorn. *Directions:* The village of Tasch is your final destination. The hotel can reserve covered parking. The staff will take care of your luggage and organize the transfer from Tasch to your hotel, either by taxi or train. Be sure to call ahead for reservations.

SEILER HOTEL MONT CERVIN
Manager: Wolfgang Pinkwart
Bahnhofstrasse 31, Postfach 210
CH-3920 Zermatt, Switzerland
Tel: (027) 966 88 88, Fax: (027) 966 88 99
128 rooms, Double: CHF 380–CHF 1380
Open: Dec to mid-Apr & mid-Jun to mid-Oct
Credit cards: all major
In the center of Zermatt, Train: 5-minute walk
Region: Valais
karenbrown.com/switzerland/seilerhotelmontcervin.html

The Hotel Monte Rosa is a must when evaluating the hotels of Zermatt. How could you possibly not consider the original hotel in Zermatt, one that is so intricately interwoven with the history of this wonderful old village? The members of the Seiler family who own the Monte Rosa are descendants of Alexander Seiler who waved goodbye on July 13, 1865, to the famous Englishman, Edward Whymper, as he began his historic climb to become the first man to conquer the Matterhorn. Back in the 1800s, when Edward Whymper was asked about the best hotel in Zermatt, he always replied, "Go to the Monte Rosa—go to Seiler's." The answer has not changed over the past century. There are now several Seiler hotels on the hotel scene, but it is still the Monte Rosa that best captures the nostalgia of the old Zermatt. It is not just the romance that makes this inn so special—it also has delightful old-world lounges such as the pine-paneled Whymper Room and the traditional billiard room, and lovely guestrooms all tastefully decorated in an old-world style. Each bedroom is lovely in its own way, with fine furnishings accented by pretty, color-coordinated fabrics. The service is refined and reflects the best in Swiss tradition and hospitality. Guests loyally return year after year to experience this exceptional hotel. *Directions:* Park you car by the train station in Tasch, take the train to Zermatt, and your hotel electric car will be waiting at the station.

SEILER HOTEL MONTE ROSA
Manager: Martin Sonderegger
Bahnofstrasse 80, P.O. Box 220
CH-3920 Zermatt, Switzerland
Tel: (027) 966 03 33, Fax: (027) 966 03 30
47 rooms, Double: CHF 294–CHF 760
Open: mid-Dec to mid-Apr & mid-Jun to mid-Oct
Credit cards: all major
In the center of Zermatt, Train: 5-minute walk
Region: Valais
karenbrown.com/switzerland/seilerhotelmonterosa.html

The Claridge Hotel Tiefenau is a real charmer, an appealing country inn away from the bustle of the city, yet within easy walking distance of the heart of Zürich. Lacy trees frame the yellow façade whose small-paned windows are enhanced by off-white shutters. A gay yellow-and-white striped awning forms a cozy canopy over the front entry. From the moment you enter, you are surrounded by a homey ambiance—nothing commercial, just comfortable chairs, antique chests, Oriental rugs, lovely paintings, and sunlight streaming in through the many windows. The bedrooms are a special surprise. Each seems so large as to almost be a suite, with plenty of space to relax and read or write letters (all the rooms even have fax/modem hook-ups). The newly renovated, à-la-carte restaurant, Züri-Stube, specializes in local cooking with a large variety of local Zürich wines. In warm weather, meals are served outside in a delightful little garden tucked against the side of the hotel. The cozy Orson's Restaurant and Bar serves Euro-Asian specialties. Beat Blumer owns and personally manages the Tiefenau. *Directions:* From the train station, cross over the Limmat River on Bahnhofbrücke, turn right on Hirschengraben, which becomes Zeltweg after it crosses Rämistrasse, and then turn left on Steinwiesstrasse.

CLARIDGE HOTEL TIEFENAU
Owner: Beat Blumer
Steinwiesstrasse 8-10
CH-8032 Zürich, Switzerland
Tel: (01) 267 87 87, Fax: (01) 251 24 76
31 rooms, Double: CHF 260–CHF 540*
*Breakfast not included: CHF 24
Open: Jan 6 to Dec 17, Credit cards: all major
City center near the Museum of Fine Art, Train: 1 km
Region: Zürich
karenbrown.com/switzerland/hoteltiefenau.html

We discovered this charming boutique hotel when taking an evening stroll up from the river. Enchanted just by peeking through windows, we knew our brazen efforts were rewarded when we entered the lobby. The Hotel Kindli, once a 16th-century townhouse, retains the warmth and character of a private home. Decorated throughout in Laura Ashley wallpapers and fabrics, the guestrooms are rich and handsome in their furnishings. The setting, on cobbled streets at the heart of the pedestrian district, affords quiet and a wonderful central location. Rooms open to the sounds of footsteps on cobbled streets and the bells of St. Peter's. Since it was evening and many guests had already checked in, we felt fortunate to see even a sampling of rooms. All the rooms have private bathrooms and open off lovely quiet corridors. A circular stair of beautiful pink marble winds up through the center of the home (they also have an elevator). Everything here is tasteful and English-country, yet if you are not attracted by the rooms, you might simply find yourself a patron of the wonderful Café Restaurant Opus, which is cozy and inviting, with a piano set center stage for an evening of quiet background music. *Directions:* Located on a pedestrian area just up from the river off the Limmat Quai on the east side. Ask for directions as to where to park and how to unload your luggage.

HOTEL KINDLI
Owner: Gisela Lacher
Pfalzgasse 1
CH-8001 Zürich, Switzerland
Tel: (01) 211 59 17, Fax: (01) 211 65 28
20 rooms, Double: CHF 330–CHF 360
Open: all year, Credit cards: all major
At the heart of town, Train: 5-minute walk
Region: Zürich
karenbrown.com/switzerland/kindi.html

A small hotel more than 400 years old, the Romantik Hotel Florhof is located on the north side of the River Limmat on a quiet street that twists up from the little squares and alleys of old Zürich. Providing a tranquil oasis from the bustle of activity, but close enough for you to walk to all major attractions such as the art museum and the university, the Florhof is more like a residence than a hotel. Having been totally refurbished in 2000, it is elegant, yet comfortable and in keeping with the style of this lovely old patrician home. The outside is painted a pretty gray-blue, and there is an intimate patio at the rear—perfect for summer dining. The entry is warmed by richly paneled walls, dramatic flower arrangements, and a marvelous old blue-and-white rococo tile stove. Just off the lobby is a cozy dining room where you can enjoy delicious, market-fresh cuisine. Beautiful guestrooms are all elegantly similar, decorated in either a blue, red, or green color scheme mixed with rich creams, and have handsome antiques. Perhaps the greatest asset of the Florhof is the graciousness of its enthusiastic hosts, Brigitte and Beat Schiesser. Having traveled extensively, they have now chosen to settle in Zürich and make this charming inn their home. *Directions:* From the train station, cross over the Limmat River on Bahnhofbrücke, turn right on Hirschengraben and then left on Florhofgasse just before the Kunsthaus.

ROMANTIK HOTEL FLORHOF
Owners: Brigitte & Beat Schiesser
Florhofgasse 4
CH-8001 Zürich, Switzerland
Tel: (01) 261 44 70, Fax: (01) 261 46 11
35 rooms, Double: CHF 360–CHF 580
Open: all year, Credit cards: all major
Walking distance of heart of Zürich, Train: 10-min walk
Region: Zürich
karenbrown.com/switzerland/romantikhotelflorhof.html

The Hotel zum Storchen is absolutely wonderful, offering the professional service of a grand hotel but with a truly personal touch. How often in a city hotel is an invitation extended to take a 6:30 morning sightseeing jog with the hotel's charming director? Under Jean Philippe Jaussi's direction, the staff not only serves graciously but seems to anticipate one's needs. Guests enjoy the most sophisticated luxuries in modern bedrooms, all beautifully decorated in rich fabrics of reds, blues, and creams that complement the handsome walnut and mahogany furniture. A few rooms deserve special mention: Room 323 is a favorite, a large corner room with an expanse of river view through French windows, and 521, although a standard room, enjoys a private terrace overlooking the rooftops of town. The Storchen Bar is a cozy place to settle for a drink and accompanying piano music. The dining room is elegant, with an excellent menu and wonderful views (weather permitting, tables are set on the geranium-adorned terrace). The dining room is also the stage for a breakfast feast of juices, breads, meats, cheeses, cereals, and yogurts. Recent renovations have dramatically enhanced the entry and lobby of the hotel. Zürich is one of Europe's most elegant cities, and the Zum Storchen affords a comfortably elegant base. *Directions:* From the Lucerne highway follow Zürich City/See signs and turn left before the bridge.

HOTEL ZUM STORCHEN
Director: J. Philippe Jaussi
Am Weinplatz 2
CH-8001 Zürich, Switzerland
Tel: (01) 227 27 27, Fax: (01) 227 27 00
75 rooms, Double: CHF 520–CHF 950
Open: all year, Credit cards: all major
On the banks of the River Limmat, Train: 1.5 km
Region: Zürich
karenbrown.com/switzerland/hotelzumstorchen.html

Cantons of Switzerland

Key Map of Switzerland

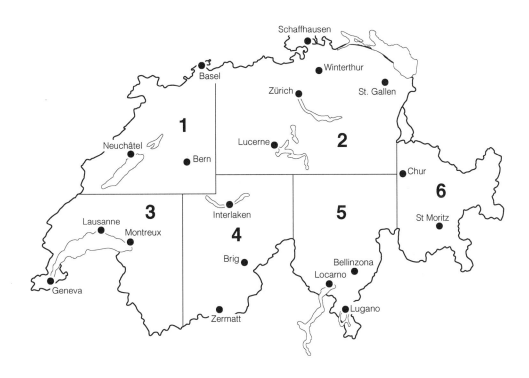

Map 1

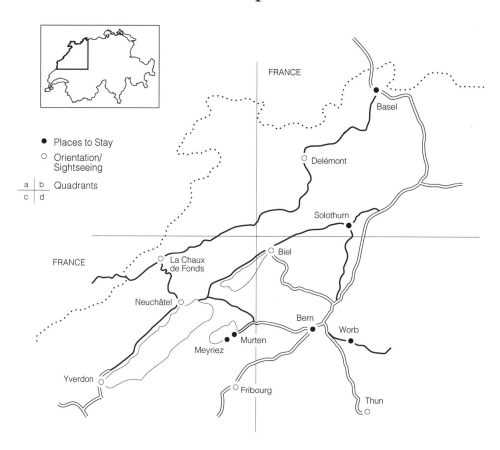

- ● Places to Stay
- ○ Orientation/ Sightseeing

a	b
c	d

Quadrants

FRANCE

Basel

Delémont

Solothurn

FRANCE

Biel

La Chaux de Fonds

Neuchâtel

Bern

Worb

Meyriez

Murten

Yverdon

Fribourg

Thun

Map 2

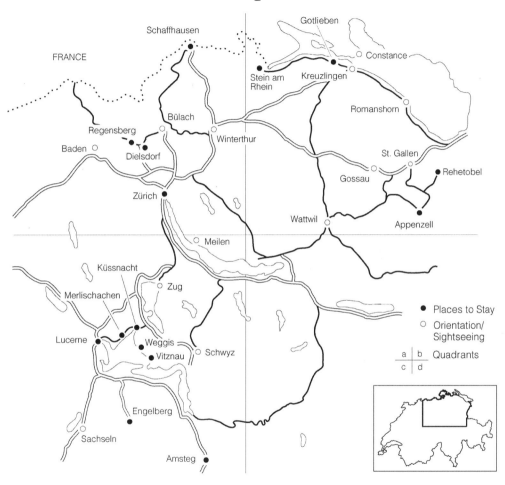

FRANCE

Schaffhausen

Gotlieben

Constance

Stein am Rhein

Kreuzlingen

Romanshorn

Bülach

Winterthur

Regensberg

Baden

Dielsdorf

St. Gallen

Rehetobel

Gossau

Zürich

Wattwil

Appenzell

Meilen

Küssnacht

Zug

Merlischachen

Lucerne

Weggis

Schwyz

Vitznau

Engelberg

Sachseln

Amsteg

● Places to Stay

○ Orientation/ Sightseeing

| a | b | Quadrants |
| c | d | |

233

Map 3

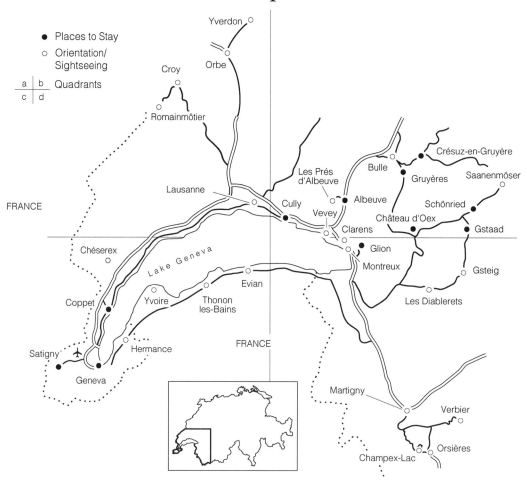

- ● Places to Stay
- ○ Orientation/ Sightseeing

a	b
c	d

Quadrants

Yverdon

Orbe

Croy

Romainmôtier

Les Prés d'Albeuve

Crésuz-en-Gruyère

Bulle

Gruyères

Saanenmöser

Lausanne

Cully

Albeuve

FRANCE

Vevey

Schönried

Château d'Oex

Clarens

Gstaad

Glion

Chéserex

Montreux

Gsteig

Lake Geneva

Evian

Les Diablerets

Coppet

Yvoire

Thonon les-Bains

Satigny

Hermance

FRANCE

Geneva

Martigny

Verbier

Orsières

Champex-Lac

234

Map 4

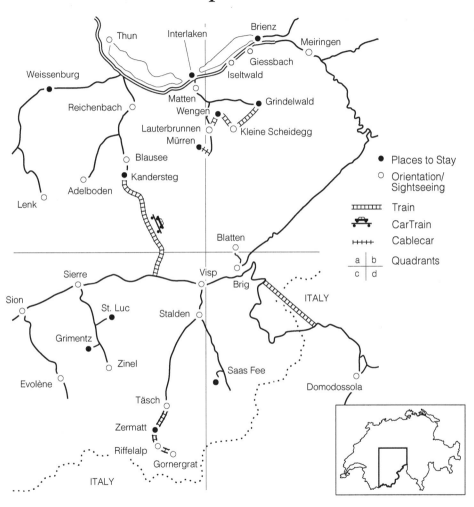

Thun

Interlaken

Brienz

Meiringen

Weissenburg

Giessbach

Iseltwald

Reichenbach

Matten

Grindelwald

Wengen

Lauterbrunnen

Kleine Scheidegg

Mürren

Blausee

● Places to Stay

○ Orientation/
   Sightseeing

Adelboden

Kandersteg

🚃 Train

🚗 CarTrain

Lenk

Blatten

┼┼┼┼ Cablecar

a	b
c	d

Quadrants

Visp

Sierre

Sion

Brig

ITALY

St. Luc

Stalden

Grimentz

Zinel

Saas Fee

Evolène

Domodossola

Täsch

Zermatt

Riffelalp

Gornergrat

ITALY

Map 5

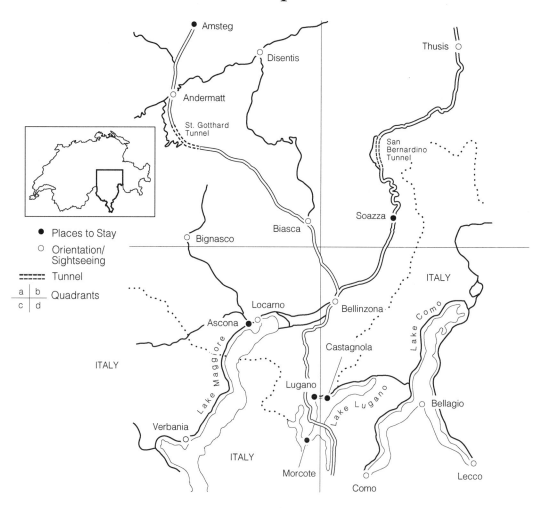

Amsteg

Disentis

Thusis

Andermatt

St. Gotthard
Tunnel

San
Bernardino
Tunnel

Soazza

Biasca

Bignasco

ITALY

● Places to Stay
○ Orientation/
   Sightseeing
===== Tunnel

a	b
c	d

Quadrants

Locarno

Bellinzona

Ascona

Castagnola

ITALY

Lugano

Bellagio

Verbania

Morcote

ITALY

Como

Lecco

Map 6

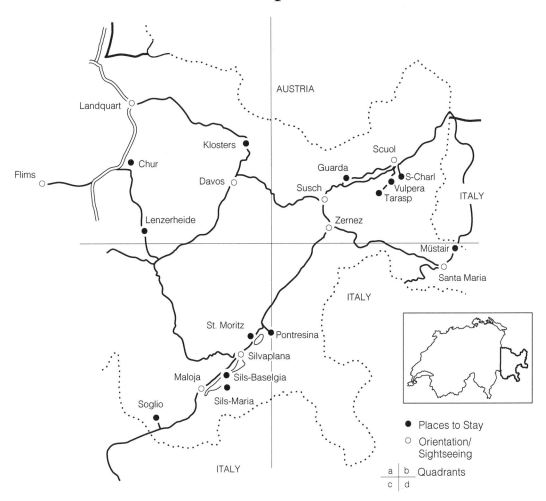

Landquart

AUSTRIA

Klosters

Chur

Flims

Davos

Scuol

Guarda

Susch

S-Charl

Vulpera

Tarasp

ITALY

Lenzerheide

Zernez

Müstair

Santa Maria

ITALY

St. Moritz

Pontresina

Silvaplana

Maloja

Sils-Baselgia

Soglio

Sils-Maria

ITALY

● Places to Stay

○ Orientation/
  Sightseeing

a	b
c	d

Quadrants

237

Index

Index

Index

Zug, 61
    Sightseeing, 58
Zuger-See, 61
Zum Storchen (Hotel), Zürich, 111, 122, 228
Zürich, 85, 111, 122
    Claridge Hotel Tiefenau, 111, 122, 225
    Kindli (Hotel), 111, 122, 226
    Romantik Hotel Florhof, 111, 122, 227
    Sightseeing, 58
    Zum Storchen (Hotel), 111, 122, 228

Enhance your Guides—Visit us Online

www.karenbrown.com

- Hotel specials
- Color photos of hotels and B&Bs
- 20% online discount for book purchases
- Discount airfare, both business and coach class
- Direct links to individual property websites and e-mails
- Up-to-the-minute phone, fax, and e-mail information
- Rental cars, travel planning, trip insurance, itineraries, maps, and more

Become a Member of the Karen Brown Club

- Additional specials and offers from our travel partners
- Exclusive access to "new discoveries" from our current research
- An additional 20% savings on purchases from our online store

A complete listing of member benefits can be found on our website

Don't delay, join online today!

www.karenbrown.com

destination ∞ europe

Karen Brown's

Preferred Provider of

Discount Air Travel to Europe

Coach- and Business-Class Tickets

Regularly Scheduled Flights on Major International Carriers

Service to 200 Gateway Destination Cities

Additional 5% off Published Fares in 2004
for Karen Brown Travelers

800-223-5555

Be sure to identify yourself as a Karen Brown Traveler
For special offers and discounts use your

Karen Brown ID number 99006187

Make reservations online via our website, www.karenbrown.com
Click "Discount Airfares" on our home page or call 800-223-5555

Providing unforgettable
introductions to
the finest accommodations
and hospitality
in North America
for over thirty years.
Each property is inspected
for quality assurance
and meets the
exceptional standards
set by the
Association
and its members.

SELECT REGISTRY

DISTINGUISHED INNS OF NORTH AMERICA

www.SelectRegistry.com
800.344.5244

KB Travel Service

❖ **KB Travel Service** offers travel-planning assistance using itineraries designed by *Karen Brown* and published in her guidebooks. We will customize any itinerary to fit your personal interests.

❖ We will plan your itinerary with you, help you decide how long to stay and what to do once you arrive, and work out the details.

❖ We will book your airline tickets and your rental car, arrange rail travel, reserve accommodations recommended in *Karen Brown's Guides,* and supply you with point-to-point information and consultation.

Contact us to start planning your travel!

800-782-2128 or e-mail: info@kbtravelservice.com

Service fees do apply

KB Travel Service
16 East Third Avenue
San Mateo, CA 94401 USA
www.kbtravelservice.com

Independently owned and operated by Town & Country Travel
CST 2001543-10

Seal Cove Inn

Located in the San Francisco Bay Area

Karen Brown Herbert (best known as author of Karen Brown's Guides) and her husband, Rick, have put 23 years of experience into reality and opened their own superb hideaway, Seal Cove Inn. Spectacularly set amongst wildflowers and bordered by towering cypress trees, Seal Cove Inn looks out to the distant ocean over acres of county park: an oasis where you can enjoy secluded beaches, explore tide-pools, watch frolicking seals, and follow the tree-lined path that traces the windswept ocean bluffs. Country antiques, original watercolors, flower-laden cradles, rich fabrics, and the gentle ticking of grandfather clocks create the perfect ambiance for a foggy day in front of the crackling log fire. Each bedroom is its own haven with a cozy sitting area before a wood-burning fireplace and doors opening onto a private balcony or patio with views to the park and ocean. Moss Beach is a 35-minute drive south of San Francisco, 6 miles north of the picturesque town of Half Moon Bay, and a few minutes from Princeton harbor with its colorful fishing boats and restaurants. Seal Cove Inn makes a perfect base for whale watching, salmon-fishing excursions, day trips to San Francisco, exploring the coast, or, best of all, just a romantic interlude by the sea, time to relax and be pampered. Karen and Rick look forward to the pleasure of welcoming you to their coastal hideaway.

Seal Cove Inn • 221 Cypress Avenue • Moss Beach • California • 94038 • USA
tel: (650) 728-4114, fax: (650) 728-4116, website: www.sealcoveinn.com

KAREN BROWN wrote her first travel guide in 1976. Her personalized travel series has grown to 17 titles, which Karen and her small staff work diligently to keep updated. Karen, her husband, Rick, and their children, Alexandra and Richard, live in Moss Beach, a small town on the coast south of San Francisco. They settled here in 1991 when they opened Seal Cove Inn. Karen is frequently traveling but when she is home, in her role as innkeeper, enjoys welcoming Karen Brown readers.

CLARE BROWN was a travel consultant for many years, specializing in planning itineraries to Europe using charming small hotels in the countryside. The focus of her job remains unchanged, but now her expertise is available to a larger audience—the readers of her daughter Karen's country inn guides. When Clare and her husband, Bill, are not traveling, they live either in Hillsborough, California, or at their home in Vail, Colorado, where family and friends frequently join them for skiing.

JUNE EVELEIGH BROWN'S love of travel was inspired by the *National Geographic* magazines that she read as a girl in her dentist's office—so far she has visited over 40 countries. June hails from Sheffield, England and lived in Zambia and Canada before moving to northern California where she lives in San Mateo with her husband, Tony, their daughter Clare, their two German Shepherds, and a Siamese cat.

JANN POLLARD, the artist responsible for the beautiful painting on the cover of this guide, has studied art since childhood, and is well known for her outstanding impressionistic-style watercolors, which she has exhibited in numerous juried shows, winning many awards. Jann travels frequently to Europe (using Karen Brown's Guides) where she loves to paint historical buildings. Jann's original paintings are represented through The Gallery, Burlingame, CA, 650-347-9392 or www.thegalleryart.net. Fine-art giclée prints of the cover paintings are also available at www.karenbrown.com.

BARBARA TAPP, the talented artist who produces all of the hotel sketches and delightful illustrations in this guide, was raised in Australia where she studied in Sydney at the School of Interior Design. Although Barbara continues with freelance projects, she devotes much of her time to illustrating the Karen Brown guides. Barbara lives in Kensington, California, with her husband, Richard, and daughter, Georgia.

Travel Your Dreams • Order Your Karen Brown Guides Today

Please ask in your local bookstore for Karen Brown's Guides. If the books you want are unavailable, you may order directly from the publisher. Books will be shipped immediately.

_____ *Austria: Charming Inns & Itineraries* $19.95

_____ *California: Charming Inns & Itineraries* $19.95

_____ *England: Charming Bed & Breakfasts* $18.95

_____ *England, Wales & Scotland: Charming Hotels & Itineraries* $19.95

_____ *France: Charming Bed & Breakfasts* $18.95

_____ *France: Charming Inns & Itineraries* $19.95

_____ *Germany: Charming Inns & Itineraries* $19.95

_____ *Ireland: Charming Inns & Itineraries* $19.95

_____ *Italy: Charming Bed & Breakfasts* $18.95

_____ *Italy: Charming Inns & Itineraries* $19.95

_____ *Mexico: Charming Inns & Itineraries* $19.95

_____ *Mid-Atlantic: Charming Inns & Itineraries* $19.95

_____ *New England: Charming Inns & Itineraries* $19.95

_____ *Pacific Northwest: Charming Inns & Itineraries* $19.95

_____ *Portugal: Charming Inns & Itineraries* $19.95

_____ *Spain: Charming Inns & Itineraries* $19.95

_____ *Switzerland: Charming Inns & Itineraries* $19.95

Name _____ Street _____

Town _____ State_____ Zip _____ Tel _____

Credit Card (MasterCard or Visa) _____ Expires: _____

For orders in the USA, add $5 for the first book and $2 for each additional book for shipment. Overseas shipping (airmail) is $10 for 1 to 2 books, $20 for 3 to 4 books etc. CA residents add 8.25% sales tax. Fax or mail form with check or credit card information to:

KAREN BROWN'S GUIDES
Post Office Box 70 • San Mateo • California • 94401 • USA
tel: (650) 342-9117, fax: (650) 342-9153, e-mail: karen@karenbrown.com, www.karenbrown.com

Icons Key

We have introduced the icons listed below in the guidebooks and on our website (*www.karenbrown.com*). These allow us to provide additional information about our recommended properties. When using our website to supplement the guides, placing the cursor over an icon will in many cases give you further details.

❄	Air conditioning in rooms	🍴	Restaurant
⛱	Beach	❀	Spa
☕	Breakfast included in room rate	🏊	Swimming pool
	Children welcome	🏃	Tennis
	Cooking classes offered		Television w/ English channels
CREDIT	Credit cards accepted		Wedding facilities
☎	Direct-dial telephone in room	♿	Wheelchair friendly
🐕	Dogs by special request		Golf course nearby
	Elevator	👫	Hiking trails nearby
	Exercise room	🐎	Horseback riding nearby
Y	Mini-refrigerator in room		Skiing nearby
🚭	Some non-smoking rooms		Water sports nearby
P	Parking available		Wineries nearby